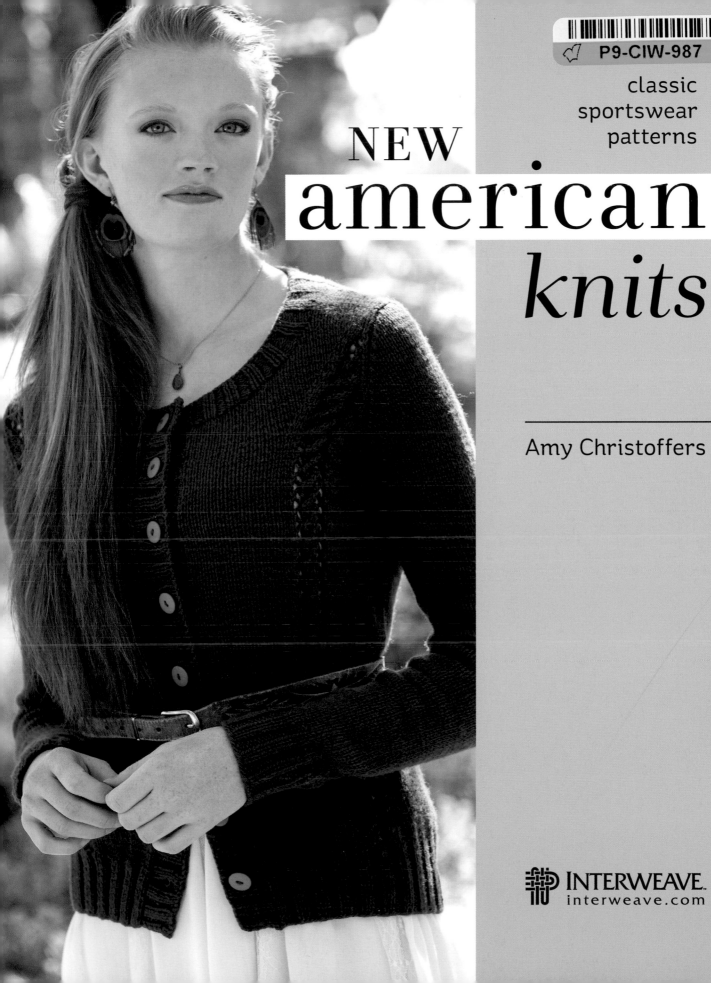

P9-CIW-987

classic
sportswear
patterns

NEW
american
knits

Amy Christoffers

INTERWEAVE.
interweave.com

Editor
Erica Smith

Technical Editor
Kristen TenDyke

Photographer
Joe Hancock

Stylists
Emily Smoot & Annie Rocchio

Hair & Makeup
Jessica Shinyeda & Kathy MacKay

Associate Art Director
Julia Boyles

Cover & Interior Design
Adrian Newman

Production Designer
Katherine Jackson

© 2014 Amy Christoffers

Photography © 2014 Joe Hancock

All rights reserved.

Interweave
A division of F+W Media, Inc.
4868 Innovation Drive
Fort Collins, CO 80525
interweave.com

Manufactured in China
by RR Donnelley Shenzhen.

Library of Congress Cataloging-in-Publication Data
Christoffers, Amy.
New American knits : 20 classic sportswear patterns / Amy Christoffers.
    pages cm
Includes index.
ISBN 978-1-62033-099-9 (pbk.)
ISBN 978-1-62033-116-3 (PDF)
1. Knitting--Patterns. I. Title.
TT825.C423127 2014
746.43'2--dc23
2013049304

10 9 8 7 6 5 4 3 2 1

For LC, the apple of my eye

contents

Introduction

THE "AMERICAN LOOK" IS SIMPLE AND PRACTICAL.
The term comes from the style of the 1930s
and 1940s–the moment in fashion when
American designers stopped looking to
Europe for inspiration and created a style that
was uniquely their own. The American Look is
fresh and modern, even by today's standards:
tailored and unfussy but with whimsical
details. Think Katharine Hepburn or Lauren
Bacall looking relaxed and casual, crisp and
tailored, all at the same time.

New American Knits is about applying
traditional knitting skills and textile motifs to
contemporary wearable knitting. It is nostalgic
but not vintage, with textures and colorwork
motifs adapted and applied with an eye
toward creating a modern wardrobe.

It is my hope that this collection reflects
how we dress every day: contemporary
sportswear, the simple-but-sophisticated
modern uniform. These pieces have clean lines
that make for soothing knitting. They feature
both seamless and semiseamless construction
and simple stitches such as garter, stockinette,
and waffle, punctuated with lace and pops of
colorwork. These pieces are engaging to knit
but not complicated, emphasizing the use
of traditional motifs, techniques, and skills
to produce a result that is satisfying in both
form and function.

I've named each of the pieces
after an American artist that
I find particularly inspiring.
I hope you are intrigued
enough to investigate them!

georgia SWEATER

FINISHED SIZE

About 36 (37½, 40¾, 44, 47¼, 51¼)" (91.5 [95.5, 103.5, 112, 120, 130] cm) bust circumference.

Pullover shown measures 36" (91.5 cm).

YARN

Sportweight (#2 fine).

SHOWN HERE: Fibre Company Savannah (50% wool, 20% cotton, 15% soya, 15% linen; 160 yd [146 m]/50 g): Cabernet (MC), 6 (7, 7, 8, 8, 9) skeins; Persimmon (CC), 1 skein.

NEEDLES

BODY—Size U.S. 6 (4 mm): 16" (40 cm) and 24" (60 cm) circular (cir) and set of 4 or 5 double-pointed (dpn).

RIBBING—Size U.S. 4 (3.5 mm): 16" (40 cm) and 24" (60 cm) cir and set of 4 or 5 dpn.

Adjust needle sizes if necessary to obtain the correct gauge.

NOTIONS

Stitch markers (m); stitch holders or waste yarn; tapestry needle; size US 7/4.5 mm crochet hook for embroidery; tailor's chalk (optional).

GAUGE

20 sts and 28 rnds = 4" (10 cm) in St st worked in rnds on larger needles.

This classic raglan sweater, named for painter Georgia O'Keefe, is given bohemian drama and interest with an oversize focal flower. The crochet slip-stitch embroidery, inspired by the hippie style of my Vermont childhood, is beautiful but optional; you can work as much or as little of it as you like. The sweater is a blank canvas for creative expression.

Stitch Guide
2×2 Rib (multiple of 4 sts)
RND 1: *K1, p2, k1; rep from *.

Rep Rnd 1 for patt.

NOTE: *Working the slipped stitch crochet is easier with a little practice. Experiment with different hook sizes on the swatch until you're confident to proceed on the completed sweater.*

Sleeve

With MC and smaller needle, CO 40 (40, 44, 44, 48, 52) sts. Divide sts evenly over 3 or 4 dpn. Place marker (pm) for beg of rnd and join for working in the rnd, being careful not to twist sts.

Work in 2×2 rib (see Stitch Guide) until piece measures 2½" (6.5 cm) from beg.

Change to larger dpn.

Work even in St st (knit all sts, every rnd) until piece measures 4½" (11.5 cm) from beg.

Shape Sleeve

INC RND: K1, M1L (see Techniques), knit to last st, M1R (see Techniques), k1–2 sts inc'd.

Knit 11 (9, 9, 7, 6, 6) rnds.

Rep the last 12 (10, 10, 10, 7, 7) rnds 7 (9, 9, 11, 12, 13) times—56 (60, 64, 68, 74, 80) sts.

Work even in St st until piece measures 19" (48.5 cm) from beg, ending last rnd 4 (5, 6, 7, 8, 9) sts before m. Place 8 (10, 12, 14, 16, 18) sts onto st holder or waste yarn for underarm, then place rem 48 (50, 52, 54, 58, 62) sts aside for yoke. Break yarn.

Make a second sleeve the same as the first.

Body

With MC and larger cir, CO 176 (184, 200, 216, 232, 252) sts. Pm for beg of rnd and join for working in the rnd, being careful not to twist sts.

Work in 2×2 rib until piece measures 2½" (6.5 cm) from beg.

Work in St st until piece measures 5¾" (14.5 cm) from beg.

PM FOR SIDE: K88 (92, 100, 108, 116, 126) sts, pm for side, knit to end.

Shape Waist

DEC RND: *K1, k2tog, knit to 3 sts before side m, ssk, k1, sl m; rep from * once more—4 sts dec'd.

Knit 13 rnds.

Rep the last 14 rnds once more—168 (176, 192, 208, 224, 244) sts.

Knit 8 rnds.

INC RND: *K1, M1L, knit to 3 sts before side m, M1R, k1, sl m; rep from * once more—4 sts inc'd.

Knit 11 rnds.

Rep the last 12 rnds 2 times—180 (188, 204, 220, 236, 256) sts.

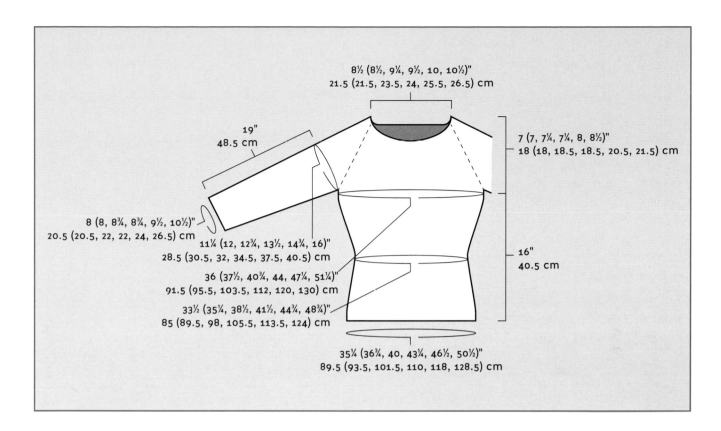

8½ (8½, 9¼, 9½, 10, 10½)"
21.5 (21.5, 23.5, 24, 25.5, 26.5) cm

19"
48.5 cm

7 (7, 7¼, 7¼, 8, 8½)"
18 (18, 18.5, 18.5, 20.5, 21.5) cm

8 (8, 8¾, 8¾, 9½, 10½)"
20.5 (20.5, 22, 22, 24, 26.5) cm

11¼ (12, 12¾, 13½, 14¾, 16)"
28.5 (30.5, 32, 34.5, 37.5, 40.5) cm

36 (37½, 40¾, 44, 47¼, 51¼)"
91.5 (95.5, 103.5, 112, 120, 130) cm

16"
40.5 cm

33½ (35¼, 38½, 41½, 44¾, 48¾)"
85 (89.5, 98, 105.5, 113.5, 124) cm

35¼ (36¾, 40, 43¼, 46½, 50½)"
89.5 (93.5, 101.5, 110, 118, 128.5) cm

Cont working even in St st until piece measures 16" (40.5 cm) from beg, ending last rnd 4 (5, 6, 7, 8, 9) sts before the beg of rnd m.

Yoke

JOINING RND: Cont working with cir holding body sts. *Place next 8 (10, 12, 14, 16, 18) sts onto st holder or waste yarn for underarm, removing m, return 48 (50, 52, 54, 58, 62) held sts from one sleeve onto empty end of cir and knit across, pm for raglan, k82 (84, 90, 96, 102, 110) sts to 4 (5, 6, 7, 8, 9) sts before side m, pm; rep from * once more—260 (268, 284, 300, 320, 344) sts. Last m placed is new beg of rnd.

Shape Raglan

DEC RND: *K1, k2tog, knit to 3 sts before next m, ssk, k1, sl m; rep from * 3 more times—8 sts dec'd.

Knit 1 rnd.

Rep the last 2 rnds 3 (4, 5, 18, 19, 22) times—228 (228, 236, 148, 160, 160) sts; 40 (40, 40, 16, 18, 16) sts each sleeve, 74 (74, 78, 58, 62, 64) sts each back and front.

Sizes 36 (37½, 40¾)" only:

[Rep dec rnd, then work 3 rnds even] 3 (2, 2) times—204 (212, 220) sts rem: 34 (36, 36) sts each sleeve, 68 (70, 74) sts each back and front.

[Rep dec rnd, then work 1 rnd even] 8 (9, 9) times—140 (140, 148) sts rem: 18 sts each sleeve, 52 (52, 56) sts each back and front.

All Sizes
Shape Raglan and Neck

NOTE: *Change to 16" (40.5 cm) cir when sts no longer fit comfortably on 24" (61 cm) cir.*

DEC RND: K1, k2tog, knit to 3 sts before next m, ssk, k1, sl m, k1, k2tog, k19 (19, 21, 21, 23, 23) sts, BO the next 8 (8, 8, 10, 10, 12) sts for front neck, knit to 3 sts before next m, ssk, k1, sl m, *k1, k2tog, knit to 3 sts before the next m, k1, sl m; rep from * once more—124 (124, 132, 130, 142, 140) sts rem: 16 (16, 16, 14, 16, 14) sts each sleeve, 50 (50, 54, 56, 60, 62) sts for back, 21 (21, 23, 23, 25, 25) sts each front.

Break yarn, then sl sts so needle tips are at the front neck BO. Join MC to cont working back and forth in rows, beg with a WS row.

NECK DEC ROW (WS): BO 5 (5, 6, 6, 6, 6) sts, purl to end—5 (5, 6, 6, 6, 6) sts dec'd.

NECK AND RAGLAN DEC ROW (RS): BO 5 (5, 6, 6, 6, 6) sts, *knit to 3 sts before next m, ssk, k1, sl m, k1, k2tog; rep from * 3 more times, knit to end—106 (106, 112, 110, 122, 120) sts: 14 (14, 14, 12, 14, 12) sts each sleeve, 48 (48, 52, 54, 58, 60) sts for back, 15 (15, 16, 16, 18, 18) sts each front.

NECK DEC ROW (WS): BO 4 (4, 4, 4, 3, 3) sts, purl to end—4 (4, 4, 4, 3, 3) sts dec'd.

NECK AND RAGLAN DEC ROW (RS): BO 4 (4, 4, 4, 3, 3) sts, *knit to 3 sts before next m, ssk, k1, sl m, k1, k2tog; rep from * 3 more times, knit to end—12 (12, 12, 12, 11, 11) sts dec'd.

Rep the last 2 rows 1 (1, 1, 1, 2, 2) times—74 (74, 80, 78, 80, 78) sts: 10 (10, 10, 8, 8, 6) sts each sleeve, 44 (44, 48, 50, 52, 54) sts for back, 5 (5, 6, 6, 6, 6) sts each front.

NECK DEC ROW (WS): BO 2 (2, 3, 2, 3, 3) sts, purl to end—2 (2, 3, 2, 3,3) sts dec'd.

NECK AND RAGLAN DEC ROW (RS): BO 2 (2, 3, 2, 3, 3) sts, *knit to 3 sts before next m, ssk, k1, sl m, k1, k2tog; rep from * 3 more times, knit to end—62 (62, 66, 66, 66, 64) sts: 8 (8, 8, 6, 6, 4) sts each sleeve, 42 (42, 46, 48, 50, 52) sts for back, 2 (2, 2, 3, 2, 2) sts each front.

BO rem sts.

Finishing

Block piece to measurements.

Return held underarm sts to dpn. Holding RS tog and WS facing out, graft sts together using Kitchener St (see Techniques).

Neckband

With CC and smaller cir, beg at left back shoulder, pick up and knit 100 (100, 108, 108, 112, 112) sts around neck edge. Pm and join for working in the rnd. Knit 5 rnds. BO all sts loosely.

Embroidery

Beg the embroidery by finding the center front and placing a mark 7" (18 cm) below the neckband edge using waste yarn or tailor's chalk. Using the mark as the center point and the photo as a guide, beg working the sl st crochet motif from the center out.

Weave in all ends. Block as desired.

neel JACKET

FINISHED SIZE

About 36½ (39½, 42½, 45½, 48½, 51½)"
(92.5 [100.5, 108, 115.5, 123, 131] cm) bust
circumference, buttoned, with 3" (7.5 cm)
overlapping buttonband.

Cardigan shown measures 36½" (92.5 cm).

YARN

Worsted weight (#4 medium).

SHOWN HERE: Imperial Yarn Erin (100% wool;
245 yd [224 m]/113 g): Rain, 5 (5, 5, 6, 6, 7)
skeins.

NEEDLES

BODY—Size U.S. 9 (5.5 mm): 24" (60 cm)
circular (cir) and set of 4 or 5 double-
pointed (dpn).

EDGING—Size U.S. 8 (5 mm): 24" (60 cm) cir
and set of 4 or 5 dpn.

*Adjust needle sizes if necessary to obtain
the correct gauge.*

NOTIONS

Movable stitch markers (m); stitch holders;
tapestry needle; two 1⅜" (3.5 cm) buttons.

GAUGE

15 sts and 26 rows = 4" (10 cm) in seed st on
smaller needles.

16 sts and 20 rows = 4" (10 cm) in Chevron
patt on larger needles.

The painter Alice Neel's portraits always
feel vintage and modern at the same time.
That timeless quality of Neel's work inspires
the textured stitch patterns and the neat,
fitted silhouette of this knitted jacket. The icy
blue-gray yarn from the Imperial Stock
Ranch is an obvious choice to match Neel's
color palette.

Stitch Guide

Seed Stitch

FLAT (MULTIPLE OF 2 STS + 1)

ROW 1 (RS): K1, *p1, k1; rep from *.

ROW 2 (WS): K1, *p1, k1; rep from *.

Rep Rows 1 and 2 for patt.

IN THE ROUND (MULTIPLE OF 2 STS)

RND 1: *K1, p1; rep from *.

RND 2: *P1, k1; rep from *.

Rep Rnds 1 and 2 for patt.

NOTES

• *Circular needles are used to accommodate a large number of stitches. Do not join; work back and forth in rows.*

• *Movable stitch markers are recommended for this project because the waist decreases are centered over the markers to keep the pattern correct throughout.*

Body

With smaller cir, CO 157 (169, 181, 193, 205, 217) sts. Do not join; work back and forth in rows.

Work in seed st (see Stitch Guide) until piece measures 4" (10 cm) from beg, ending after a RS row.

PLACE SIDE MARKERS (WS): Work 42 (45, 48, 51, 54, 57) sts for right front, work next st placing movable marker into the st on the right needle after working, work 71 (77, 83, 89, 95, 101) sts for back, work next st placing movable marker into the st on the right needle after working, work 42 (45, 48, 51, 54, 57) sts for left front.

Shape Waist

DEC ROW (RS): *Work to 1 st before the marked st, p3tog or sl1-k2tog-psso keeping in patt, replacing the m into this st; rep from * once more, work to end—4 sts dec'd.

Work 5 rows even as est.

Rep the last 6 rows 2 times—145 (157, 169, 181, 193, 205) sts.

Work 1 WS row even, removing movable markers.

Change to larger cir.

EST PATT (RS): Work 9 sts in seed st, pm for front band, work 30 (33, 36, 39, 42, 45) sts in Transition chart for right front, pm for side, cont working 67 (73, 79, 85, 91, 97) sts in Transition chart, pm for side, cont working 30 (33, 36, 39, 42, 45) sts in Transition chart for left front, pm for front band, work 9 sts in seed st.

Work 3 rows more as est.

Change Transition chart sts to Chevron chart and cont as foll:

BUTTONHOLE ROW (RS): Work 3 sts in seed st, p2tog, yo, work seed st to m, work to end as est.

Work 8 rows even as est, ending after a WS row.

INC ROW (RS): Work to first side m, M1R (see Techniques), sl m, k1, M1L (see Techniques), work to 1 st before side m, M1R, k1, sl m, M1L, work to end as est—4 sts inc'd.

Work 3 rows even, working inc'd sts into Chevron chart as they appear.

Rep the last 4 rows 2 times—157 (169, 181, 193, 205, 217) sts.

Work even as est until piece measures 15" (38 cm) from beg, ending after a WS row.

Work Buttonhole Row same as before.

Work 3 rows even as est, ending after a WS row.

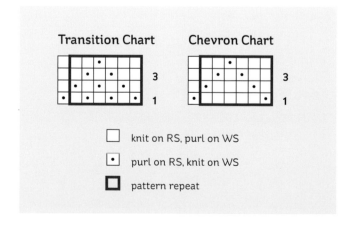

Transition Chart	Chevron Chart

☐ knit on RS, purl on WS

⊡ purl on RS, knit on WS

◻ pattern repeat

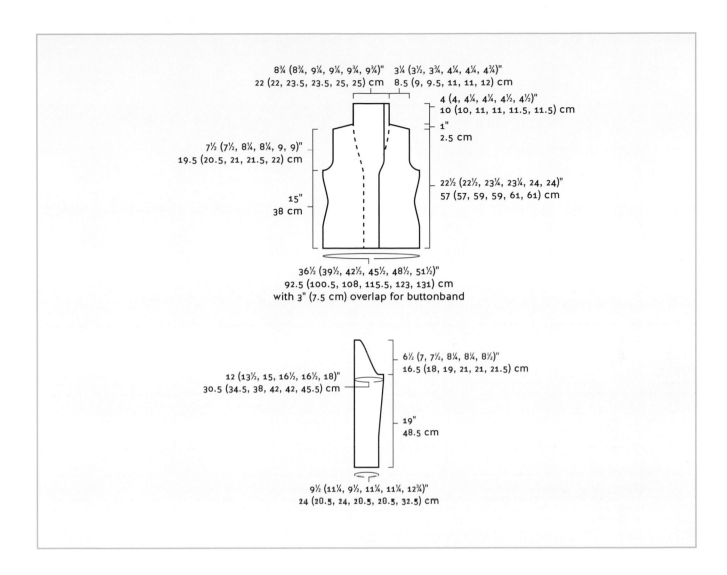

8¾ (8¾, 9¼, 9¼, 9¾, 9¾)"
22 (22, 23.5, 23.5, 25, 25) cm

3¼ (3½, 3¾, 4¼, 4¼, 4¾)"
8.5 (9, 9.5, 11, 11, 12) cm

4 (4, 4¼, 4¼, 4½, 4½)"
10 (10, 11, 11, 11.5, 11.5) cm

1"
2.5 cm

7½ (7½, 8¼, 8¼, 9, 9)"
19.5 (20.5, 21, 21.5, 22) cm

22½ (22½, 23¼, 23¼, 24, 24)"
57 (57, 59, 59, 61, 61) cm

15"
38 cm

36½ (39½, 42½, 45½, 48½, 51½)"
92.5 (100.5, 108, 115.5, 123, 131) cm
with 3" (7.5 cm) overlap for buttonband

6½ (7, 7½, 8¼, 8¼, 8½)"
16.5 (18, 19, 21, 21, 21.5) cm

12 (13½, 15, 16½, 16½, 18)"
30.5 (34.5, 38, 42, 42, 45.5) cm

19"
48.5 cm

9½ (11¼, 9½, 11¼, 11¼, 12¾)"
24 (20.5, 24, 20.5, 20.5, 32.5) cm

Divide Fronts and Back

Work 39 (41, 43, 45, 47, 49) sts for right front, BO the next 7 (9, 11, 13, 15, 17) sts, removing m, work 67 (71, 75, 79, 83, 87) sts for back, BO the next 7 (9, 11, 13, 15, 17) sts, removing m, work rem 39 (41, 43, 45, 47, 49) sts for left front.

Cont working back and forth on left front sts only. Place sts for back and right front onto st holder or waste yarn.

Left Front
Shape Armhole and Front Band

Work 1 WS row even as est.

SHAPING ROW (RS): K1, k2tog, work as est to m, sl m, M1R or M1p (see Techniques) keeping in patt, work in seed st to end.

Rep the last 2 rows, 2 (3, 3, 3, 4, 4) times, working the inc'd sts in seed st as they appear and keeping 2 sts at armhole edge in St st (knit on RS, purl on WS) throughout—39 (41, 43, 45, 47, 49) total sts: 12 (13, 13, 13, 14, 14) band sts and 27 (28, 30, 32, 33, 35) left front sts.

Shape Front Band

Work 1 WS row even as est.

SHAPING ROW (RS): Work as est to 3 sts before m, ssk, k1 (keep this st in St st throughout), sl m, M1R or M1p keeping in patt, work in seed st to end.

Rep the last 2 rows 4 (3, 3, 3, 2, 2) times—39 (41, 43, 45, 47, 49) total sts: 17 band sts and 22 (24, 26, 28, 30, 32) left front sts.

Shape Neck

Work 1 WS row even as est.

DEC ROW (RS): Work as est to 3 sts before m, ssk, k1, sl m, work in seed st to end—1 st dec'd.

Rep the last 2 rows 6 (7, 8, 8, 10, 10) times—32 (33, 34, 36, 36, 38) total sts rem: 17 band sts and 15 (16, 17, 19, 19, 21) left front sts.

Work even as est until armhole measures about 7½ (7½, 8¼, 8¼, 9, 9)" (19 [19, 21, 21, 23, 23] cm) from divide, ending after WS Row 4 of patt. Discontinue Chevron chart and cont working left front sts in St st instead; maintain front band sts in seed st.

Work 1 RS row even as established.

Shape Shoulders with Short-Rows (see Techniques)

SHORT-ROW 1 (WS): Work to last 4 (5, 5, 6, 6, 6) sts, wrap next st, and turn so RS is facing. Work 1 RS row.

SHORT-ROW 2 (WS): Work to last 8 (10, 10, 12, 12, 12) sts, wrap next st, and turn so RS is facing. Work 1 RS row.

NEXT ROW (WS): Work to end, picking up the wraps and working them together with the sts they wrap as they appear.

NEXT ROW (RS): K13 (14, 15, 17, 17, 19) sts and place them onto a st holder or waste yarn for shoulder, work rem 19 sts in seed st for neck extension.

Neck Extension

Work even until piece measures 4 (4, 4¼, 4¼, 4½, 4½)" (10 [10, 11, 11, 11.5, 11.5] cm) from held shoulder sts, gently stretched. Place live sts onto a st holder or waste yarn. Break yarn.

Back

Return 67 (71, 75, 79, 83, 87) held back sts to larger cir and join yarn, preparing to work a WS row.

Shape Armholes

Work 1 WS row even as est.

DEC ROW (RS): K1, k2tog, work as est to last 3 sts, ssk, k1–2 sts dec'd.

Rep the last 2 rows 2 (3, 3, 3, 4, 4) times, keeping the first and last 2 sts in St st throughout—61 (63, 67, 71, 73, 77) sts rem.

Work as est until armholes measure about 7½ (7½, 8¼, 8¼, 9, 9)" (19 [19, 21, 21, 23, 23] cm) from divide, ending after WS Row 4 of patt. Discontinue Chevron chart and cont working in St st.

Shape Shoulders with Short-Rows

SHORT-ROW 1 (RS): Knit to last 4 (5, 5, 6, 6, 6) sts, wrap next st, and turn so WS is facing; (WS) purl to last 4 (5, 5, 6, 6, 6) sts, wrap next st, and turn so RS is facing.

SHORT-ROW 2 (RS): Knit to last 8 (10, 10, 12, 12, 12) sts, wrap next st, and turn so WS is facing; (WS) purl to last 8 (10, 10, 12, 12, 12) sts, wrap next st, and turn so RS is facing.

NEXT ROW (RS): Knit to end, picking up the wraps and working them together with the sts they wrap as they appear.

Shape Neck

NEXT ROW (WS): P13 (14, 15, 17, 17, 19) sts, BO the next 35 (35, 37, 37, 39, 39) sts, p13 (14, 15, 17, 17, 19) to end, picking up the wraps and working them together with the sts they wrap as they appear. Break yarn and place rem sts onto a st holder or waste yarn.

Right Front

Return 39 (41, 43, 45, 47, 49) held right front sts to larger cir and join yarn, preparing to work a WS row.

Shape Armhole and Front Band

Work 1 WS row even as est.

SHAPING ROW (RS): Work in seed st to m, M1L or M1p keeping in patt, sl m, work as est to last 3 sts, ssk, k1.

Rep the last 2 rows 2 (3, 3, 3, 4, 4) times, working the inc'd sts in seed st as they appear and keeping 2 sts at armhole edge in St st throughout—39 (41, 43, 45, 47, 49) total sts: 12 (13, 13, 13, 14, 14) band sts and 27 (28, 30, 32, 33, 35) right front sts.

Shape Front Band

Work 1 WS row even as est.

SHAPING ROW (RS): Work in seed st to m, M1L or M1p keeping in patt, sl m, k1, k2tog, work to end as est.

Rep the last 2 rows 4 (3, 3, 3, 2, 2) times—39 (41, 43, 45, 47, 49) total sts: 17 band sts and 22 (24, 26, 28, 30, 32) right front sts.

Shape Neck

Work 1 WS row even as est.

DEC ROW (RS): Work in seed st to m, sl m, k1, k2tog, work to end as est.

Rep the last 2 rows 6 (7, 8, 8, 10, 10) times—32 (33, 34, 36, 36, 38) total sts rem: 17 band sts and 15 (16, 17, 19, 19, 21) right front sts.

Work even as est until armhole measures about 7½ (7½, 8¼, 8¼, 9, 9)" (19 [19, 21, 21, 23, 23] cm) from divide, ending after WS Row 4 of patt. Discontinue Chevron chart and cont working left front sts in St st instead; maintain front band sts in seed st.

Shape Shoulders with Short-Rows

SHORT-ROW 1 (RS): Work to last 4 (5, 5, 6, 6, 6) sts, wrap next st, and turn so WS is facing. Work 1 WS row.

SHORT-ROW 2 (RS): Work to last 8 (10, 10, 12, 12, 12) sts, wrap next st, and turn so WS is facing. Work 1 WS row.

NEXT ROW (RS): Work to end, picking up the wraps and working them together with the sts they wrap as they appear.

NEXT ROW (WS): P13 (14, 15, 17, 17, 19) sts and place them onto a st holder or waste yarn for shoulder, work rem 19 sts in seed st for neck extension.

Neck Extension

Work even until piece measures 4 (4, 4¼, 4¼, 4½, 4½)" (10 [10, 11, 11, 11.5, 11.5] cm) from held shoulder sts, gently stretched. Place live sts onto a st holder or waste yarn. Break yarn, leaving a tail about a yard (meter) long for grafting.

Sleeve

With smaller needle CO 36 (42, 36, 42, 42, 48) sts. Divide evenly over 3 or 4 dpn. Pm for beg of rnd and join for working in the rnd, being careful not to twist sts.

Work in seed st until piece measures 4" (10 cm) from beg, ending after Rnd 2 of patt.

Change to larger dpn.

Work Rnds 1–4 of Transition chart in the rnd, working only the 6 sts in the red rep box. Change to Chevron chart and work until piece measures 6" (15 cm) from beg.

Shape Sleeve

INC RND: M1L or M1p keeping in patt, work as est to end of rnd, M1R or M1p keeping in patt—2 sts inc'd.

Work 9 (9, 4, 4, 4, 4) rnds even.

Rep the last 10 (10, 10, 5, 5, 5) rnds 5 (5, 11, 11, 11, 11) times—48 (54, 60, 66, 66, 72) sts.

Work even as est until piece measures 19" (48.5 cm) from beg, ending after an odd-numbered rnd, and ending last rnd 3 (4, 5, 6, 7, 8) sts before m.

NEXT RND: BO 7 (9, 11, 13, 15, 17) sts and work to end as est—41 (45, 49, 53, 51, 55) sts rem. Cont working back and forth in rows as foll:

Shape Cap

Purl 1 WS row.

DEC ROW (RS): K1, k2tog, work as est to last 3 sts, ssk, k1–2 sts dec'd.

Rep the last 2 rows 2 (3, 3, 3, 4, 4) times—35 (37, 41, 45, 41, 45) sts rem.

[Work 3 rows even, then rep dec row] 3 (2, 1, 1, 2, 1) times—29 (33, 39, 43, 37, 43) sts rem.

[Work 1 WS row even, then rep dec row] 4 (6, 9, 11, 8, 11) times—21 sts rem.

DEC ROW (WS): P1, ssp, work as est to last 3 sts, p2tog, p2–2 sts dec'd.

Rep dec row on RS.

Rep the last 2 rows 2 times—9 sts rem.

BO rem sts.

Make a second sleeve the same as the first.

Finishing

Block pieces to measurements.

Join Shoulders

Return 13 (14, 15, 17, 17, 19) held sts from left front and back shoulders onto larger needle and with RS facing each other, WS facing out, join the back and front shoulders together using the three-needle BO (see Techniques). Rep for right front and back shoulders. Set in sleeves, easing the cap into place.

Join Neck Extensions

Return 19 held neck extension sts onto larger needle and join them together using the Kitchener st (see Techniques). Sew selvedge edge of neck extensions to back neck.

Sew buttons opposite buttonholes. Weave in all loose ends. Block again if desired.

rockwell HAT

FINISHED SIZE

About 17¼ (19¾)" (44 [50] cm) circumference.

Hat shown measures 17¼" (44 cm).

YARN

DK weight (#3 light).

SHOWN HERE: Fibre Company Acadia (60% merino, 20% silk, 20% alpaca; 145 yd [133 m]/50 g): Maple, 2 skeins.

NEEDLES

BODY–Size U.S. 5 (3.75 mm): 16" (40 cm) circular (cir) and set of 4 or 5 double-pointed (dpn).

RIBBING–Size U.S 3 (3.25 mm): 16" (40 cm) cir.

Adjust needle sizes if necessary to obtain the correct gauge.

NOTIONS

Stitch markers (m); cable needle (cn); tapestry needle.

GAUGE

26 sts and 32 rows = 4" (10 cm) in cable rib on smaller needles.

The acorn motif on this hat, knit in the gorgeous Acadia tweed, was inspired by Norman Rockwell's Americana. All the twists and textures are reminiscent of Tyrolean knitting, but this motif cable is actually fairly simple, with a short pattern repeat and a few relaxing resting rounds, too.

Stitch Guide

RT: Sl 1 st to cn and hold in back, k1, k1 from cn.

LT: Sl 1 st to cn and hold in front, k1, k1 from cn.

Cable Rib (multiple of 4 sts)

RND 1: *RT, p2; rep from *.

RND 2: *K2, p2; rep from *.

Rep Rnds 1 and 2 for patt.

NOTE: *On Rnd 14 of Acorn chart, the beginning of round shifts 1 stitch to the right by slipping the last stitch as indicated in the chart key. On Rnd 21 the beginning of round shifts 1 stitch to the left by slipping the first stitch of the round.*

Hat

With smaller cir, CO 112 (128) sts. Place marker (pm) for beg of rnd and join for working in the rnd, being careful not to twist sts.

Work in cable rib until piece measures 2½" (6.5 cm) from beg. At end of Rnd 2, remove m, sl 1 st purlwise with yarn in back (pwise wyb), and replace the m, shifting the beg of rnd 1 st to the left.

Change to larger cir needle.

Work Rnds 1–3 of Acorn chart.

Rep Rnds 4–23 of Acorn chart twice, then work Rnds 24–31 for crown shaping, changing to dpns when necessary—14 (16) sts rem.

Break yarn, leaving a tail at least 6" (15 cm) long.

Acorn Chart

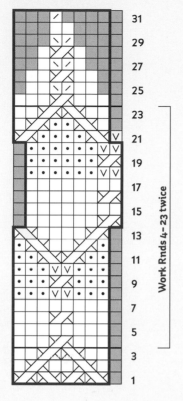

Work Rnds 4–23 twice

31
29
27
25
23
21
19
17
15
13
11
9
7
5
3
1

☐ knit

• purl

LT

RT

⋁ sl 1 st pwise wyb

LT on all repeats except at end of rnd. At end of rnd: sl 1 st to cn and hold in front, k1, sl m, place st from cn onto left needle shifting beg of rnd 1 st to the right.

⋁ Remove m, sl 1 st pwise wyb, replace m shifting beg of rnd 1 st to the left.

▨ no stitch

◿ k2tog

◺ ssk

☐ pattern repeat

Finishing

With yarn threaded onto a tapestry needle, draw tail through rem sts and cinch closed. Run the tail through the sts a few times to secure. Weave in ends. Block to measurements.

tasha SHAWL

FINISHED SIZE
About 59" (150 cm) wingspan, 29½" (75 cm) down center back.

YARN
Sportweight (#2 fine).

SHOWN HERE: Sincere Sheep Equity Sport (100% wool; 200 yd [183 m]/56 g): St. Bart's, 4 skeins.

NEEDLES
Size U.S. 6 (4 mm): 24" (60 cm) circular (cir).

Adjust needle sizes if necessary to obtain the correct gauge.

NOTIONS
Tapestry needle; blocking wires (optional); T-pins.

GAUGE
15 sts and 30 rows = 4" (10 cm) in pattern stitch, relaxed after blocking.

This shawl is meant to be a utilitarian, everyday sort of lace that works its charm in brightening up gray days. The Sincere Sheep Equity Sport is a naturally dyed 100% Rambouillet wool from Wyoming. The handspun texture of the yarn reminds me of the nostalgic illustrations of Tasha Tudor, whose books were a childhood favorite. When blocking the shawl, resist the temptation to block too much; part of the charm of this shawl is the bubbly texture of its stitch pattern, which you won't want to damp down.

Stitch Guide
M3 (K1, p1, k1) into the same st.

NOTE: *The circular needle is used to accommodate a large number of sts. Do not join; work back and forth in rows.*

Shawl

CO 1 st.

Work Rows 1–12 of Set-up chart—11 sts.

Rep Rows 1–12 of Lace chart 17 times—215 sts.

Rep Rows 1–6 of Lace chart once more—221 sts.

BO AS FOLL: BO while working M3 into each stitch across.

Finishing

Weave in ends but do not trim them yet. Soak shawl in cool water for about 20 minutes; then, using blocking wires if desired, gently stretch shawl to open up the lace and pin it into place until completely dry.

Set-up Chart

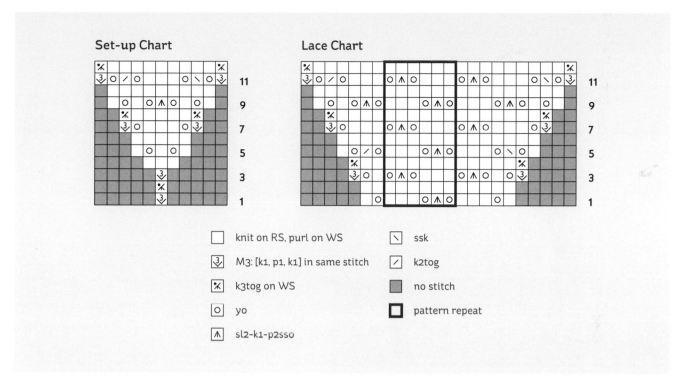

Lace Chart

knit on RS, purl on WS

☒ M3: [k1, p1, k1] in same stitch

☒ k3tog on WS

◯ yo

∧ sl2-k1-p2sso

◇ ssk

╱ k2tog

■ no stitch

▢ pattern repeat

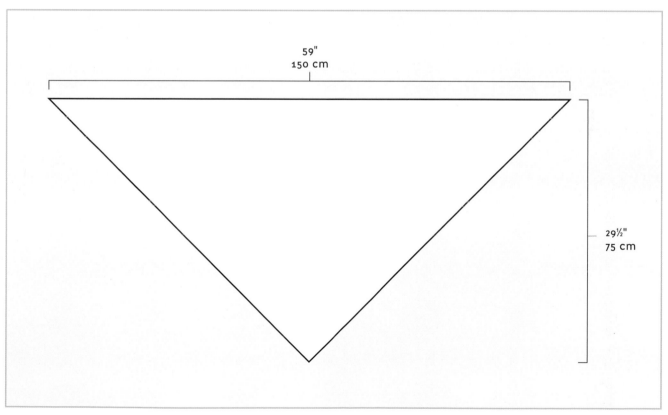

59"
150 cm

29½"
75 cm

alvarez HAT

FINISHED SIZE
About 18¼ (19¾, 20½)" (46.5 [50, 52] cm)
circumference.

Hat shown measures 18¼" (46.5 cm).

YARN
Sportweight (#2 fine).

SHOWN HERE: Harrisville New England
Shetland (100% wool; 217 yd [198 m]/50 g):
#55 pebble (MC), #19 blackberry (CC1), #65
poppy (CC2), #38 teak (CC3), #43 sand (CC4),
#54 lilac (CC5), 1 skein each.

NEEDLES
BODY—Size U.S. 3 (3.25 mm): 16" (40 cm)
circular (cir) and set of 4 or 5 double-
pointed (dpn).

RIBBING—Size U.S. 1 (2.25 mm): 16" (40 cm) cir.

*Adjust needle sizes if necessary to obtain
the correct gauge.*

NOTIONS
Stitch marker (m); tapestry needle.

GAUGE
28 sts and 28 rnds = 4" (10 cm) in Color chart
on larger needles.

This pattern recalls many of the botanical paintings of Mabel Alvarez, particularly *In the Garden*, with its bright reds, deep purples, and light browns. If knit in two colors, the motif echoes the botanical details of the seedpods; knit with six and it becomes a perennial garden. The colorwork stitch pattern follows all the rules of traditional Fair Isle: short floats, no more than two colors in a row, and symmetrical pattern repeats.

Hat

With CC1 and smaller cir, CO 128 (136, 144) sts. Place marker (pm) for beg of rnd and join for working in the rnd, being careful not to twist sts.

Break CC1 and join MC.

EST RIB: *K1, p1; rep from *.

Rep the last rnd until piece measures 2½" (6.5 cm) from beg.

Change to larger cir.

Knit 1 rnd with MC.

Work Rnds 1–43 of Color chart.

Break CC yarns and continue working with MC only.

Shape Crown

NOTE*: Change to dpn when sts no longer fit comfortably on cir needle.*

SET-UP RND: *K16 (17, 18), pm; rep from *.

DEC RND: *Knit to 2 sts before m, ssk, sl m; rep from *–8 sts dec'd.

Knit 2 rnds.

Rep the last 3 rnds 14 (15, 16) times–8 sts rem.

Break yarn, leaving a tail at least 6" (15 cm) long.

Finishing

With yarn threaded onto a tapestry needle, draw tail through rem sts and cinch closed. Run the tail through the sts a few times to secure.

Weave in ends.

Block piece to measurements.

Color Chart

Chart row numbers (right side, odd): 1, 3, 5, 7, 9, 11, 13, 15, 17, 19, 21, 23, 25, 27, 29, 31, 33, 35, 37, 39, 41, 43

Legend:
- with MC knit
- with CC1 knit
- with CC2 knit
- with CC3 knit
- with CC4 knit
- with CC5 knit

winslow CAMISOLE

FINISHED SIZE
About 32 (35½, 39, 42½, 46, 49½)" (81.5 [90, 99, 108, 117, 125.5] cm) bust circumference.

Camisole shown measures 32" (81.5 cm).

YARN
Sportweight (#2 fine).

SHOWN HERE: Classic Elite Mountain Top Vail (70% alpaca, 30% bamboo, 236 yd [216 m]/50 g): #6403 steel, 3 (4, 4, 4, 5, 5) skeins.

NEEDLES
BODY—Size U.S. 3 (3.25 mm): 24" (60 cm) circular (cir).

EDGING—Size U.S. 2 (2.5 mm): 16" (40 cm) and 24" (60 cm) cir.

Adjust needle sizes if necessary to obtain the correct gauge.

NOTIONS
Stitch markers (m); stitch holder or waste yarn; tapestry needle.

GAUGE
25 sts and 32 rnds = 4" (10 cm) in Lace chart on larger needles.

A textured vine lace pattern with garter-stitch edging pairs utility with a little sentimental sweetness, like the landscapes of the painter Winslow Homer. This camisole can be worn either as a tank or a vest. Worked in fingering-weight yarn, it works for nearly any fiber—breezy linen or cotton for summer or wool, cashmere, or silk for a light but warming winter layer.

• *Given the draping nature of the alpaca and bamboo yarn, waist shaping is optional for this project. It has been worked on the sample and included in the pattern.*

• *Because this is layering garment, a small amount of positive ease in recommended.*

• *When there are not enough stitches in a repeat remaining to work both the yarnover and the k2tog/ssk, work the stitches in St st (knit on RS, purl on WS) instead.*

• *When working the back and front in rows after dividing for the armholes, work the first and last stitches in St st throughout.*

Lace Chart

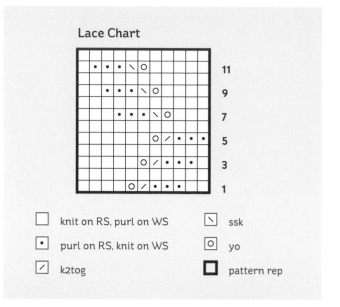

	knit on RS, purl on WS		ssk
	purl on RS, knit on WS		yo
	k2tog		pattern rep

Body

With smaller 24" (40 cm) cir, CO 200 (222, 244, 266, 288, 310) sts. Place marker (pm) and join for working in the rnd, being careful not to twist sts.

Purl 1 rnd.

Knit 1 rnd.

Rep the last 2 rnds 5 times.

Change to larger cir.

EST PATT: K1, work 11-st rep of Lace chart 9 (10, 11, 12, 13, 14) times for front, pm for side; rep from * once more for back.

Cont working even as est until piece measures 5" (12.5 cm) from beg.

Shape Waist

DEC RND: *K1, k2tog, work as est to 2 sts before side m, ssk, sl m; rep from * once more—4 sts dec'd.

Work 11 rnds even as est.

Rep the last 12 rnds 2 times— 188 (210, 232, 254, 276, 298) sts.

INC RND: *K1, M1L (see Techniques), work as est to side m, M1R (see Techniques), sl m; rep from * once more— 4 sts inc'd.

Work 11 rnds even as est.

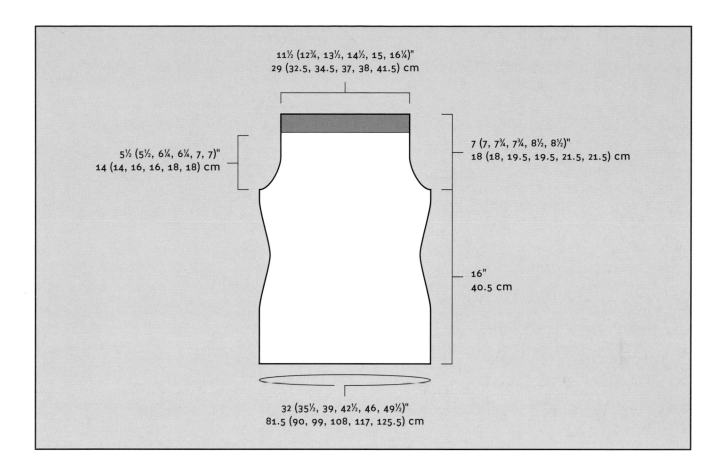

11½ (12¾, 13½, 14½, 15, 16¼)"
29 (32.5, 34.5, 37, 38, 41.5) cm

5½ (5½, 6¼, 6¼, 7, 7)"
14 (14, 16, 16, 18, 18) cm

7 (7, 7¾, 7¾, 8½, 8½)"
18 (18, 19.5, 19.5, 21.5, 21.5) cm

16"
40.5 cm

32 (35½, 39, 42½, 46, 49½)"
81.5 (90, 99, 108, 117, 125.5) cm

Rep the last 12 rnds 2 times—200 (222, 244, 266, 288, 310) sts on the needles.

Work even until piece measures about 16" (40.5 cm), ending after Rnd 6 or Rnd 12 of patt, ending last rnd 6 (6, 7, 8, 10, 11) sts before the beg of rnd m.

Divide Back and Front

NEXT RND: BO 12 (12, 14, 16, 20, 22) sts, removing m, work front to 6 (7, 8, 9, 10, 11) sts before the side m, BO 12 (14, 16, 18, 20, 22) sts, removing m, work to end for back—88 (99, 108, 117, 124, 133) sts rem each back and front.

Cont working back and forth on back sts only. Place front sts onto st holder or waste yarn.

Back

Shape Armholes

Work 1 WS row even as est.

DEC ROW (RS): K1, k2tog, work to last 3 sts, ssk, k1—2 sts dec'd.

Rep the last 2 rows 4 (5, 7, 8, 9, 10) times—78 (87, 92, 99, 104, 111) sts rem.

[Work 3 rows even, then rep dec row] 3 (4, 4, 4, 5, 5) times—72 (79, 84, 91, 94, 101) sts rem.

Work even as est until armholes measure 6 (6, 6¾, 6¾, 7½, 7½)" (15 [15, 17, 17, 19, 19] cm) from divide, ending after Row 6 or Row 12 of patt.

Change to smaller needles.

Purl the next 11 rows, ending after a WS row. BO all sts pwise.

Front

Return 88 (99, 108, 117, 124, 132) held front sts to larger needle and join yarn, preparing to work a WS row.

Shape Armholes

Work 1 WS row even as est.

DEC ROW (RS): K1, k2tog, work to last 3 sts, ssk, k1—2 sts dec'd.

Rep the last 2 rows 4 (5, 7, 8, 9, 10) times—78 (87, 92, 99, 104, 111) sts rem.

[Work 3 rows even, then rep dec row] 3 (4, 4, 4, 5, 5) times—72 (79, 84, 91, 94, 101) sts rem.

Work even as est until armholes measure 4½ (4½, 5¼, 5¼, 6, 6)" (11.5 [11.5, 13.5, 13.5, 15, 15] cm) from divide, ending after Row 6 or Row 12 of patt.

Change to smaller needles.

Purl the next 11 rows, ending after a WS row. BO all sts pwise.

Finishing

Block pieces to measurements.

Right Armhole Trim

With 16" (40 cm) cir, CO 26 sts (do not turn) with the RS facing, beg at BO edge of front right armhole, pick up and knit 89 (89, 102, 102, 116, 116) sts evenly around armhole opening—115 (115, 128, 128, 142, 142) sts. Pm for beg of rnd and join to work in the rnd, being careful not to twist CO sts.

Purl 1 rnd.

Knit 1 rnd.

Rep the last 2 rnds 4 times.

BO all sts pwise.

Left Armhole Trim

With 16" (40 cm) cir, beg at BO edge of back left armhole, pick up and knit 89 (89, 102, 102, 116, 116) sts evenly around armhole, use the cable method (see Techniques) to CO 26 sts—115 (115, 128, 128, 142, 142) sts. Pm for beg of rnd and join to work in the rnd, being careful not to twist CO sts.

Purl 1 rnd.

Knit 1 rnd.

Rep the last 2 rnds 4 times.

BO all sts pwise.

Weave in all loose ends. Block again, if desired.

wyeth SHRUG

FINISHED SIZE
About 33 (38, 43, 48)" (84 [96.5, 109, 122] cm)
wide and 35 (35, 37, 37)" (89 [89, 94, 94] cm)
high before seaming.

To fit about 33–37 (38–42, 43–47, 48–52)" (84–94
[96.5–106.5, 109–119.5, 124.5–132] cm) bust
circumference.

Shrug shown measures 38" (96.5 cm) wide
and 35" (89 cm) high before seaming.

YARN
Worsted weight (#4 medium).

SHOWN HERE: Fibre Company Terra (40%
baby alpaca, 40% merino, 20% silk, 98 yd
[90 m]/50 g): Black Locust Bark, 9 (10, 11, 12)
skeins.

NEEDLES
Size U.S. 9 (5.5 mm): 32" (80 cm) circular (cir)
and set of 4 double-pointed (dpn).

*Adjust needle sizes if necessary to obtain
the correct gauge.*

NOTIONS
A few yards of smooth waste yarn for
provisional CO and holding stitches,
movable stitch markers (m), tapestry needle.

GAUGE
15 sts and 22 rows = 4" (10 cm) in broken rib
patt.

This oversize, slouchy shrug worked in
a waffle stitch and knit-as-you-go I-cord
edging is a little deceptive in its simplicity:
worked horizontally, the seams are grafted
and the arm openings finished with an
applied I-cord. The result is a perfect balance
of refined and rustic, like the work of the
artist Andrew Wyeth.

Stitch Guide

Broken Rib (multiple of 2 sts + 7)

(also see chart)

ROW 1 (WS): Sl 3 sts purlwise with yarn in back (pwise wyb), *p1, k1; rep from * to last 4 sts, p1, k3.

ROW 2 (RS): Sl 3 sts pwise with yarn in front (wyf), purl to end.

Rep Rows 1 and 2 for patt.

Broken Rib Chart

☐ knit on RS, purl on WS

• purl on RS, knit on WS

⋎ sl pwise wyb on WS, wyf on RS

☐ pattern repeat

NOTE: *Circular needle is used to accommodate a large number of stitches. Do not join; work back and forth in rows.*

Body

With cir, use a provisional method (see Techniques) to CO 131 (131, 139, 139) sts. Do not join; work back and forth in rows.

Work in broken rib until piece measures 33 (38, 43 48)" (84 [96.5, 109, 122] cm) from beg, ending after a WS row. Break yarn leaving a tail at least 1–2 yd (0.9–1.8 m) long for grafting. Sl all sts onto waste yarn.

Finishing

Block piece to measurements.

Join Sides

Return 131 (131, 139, 139) held sts to cir. Place a movable marker after 43 (43, 45, 45) sts from each end of needle; 45 (45, 49, 49) sts are in the center of the markers.

Spread the sts out over the length of the needle and hold the tips of the needle together with RS together and WS facing out, with sts from each end of the shrug at the respective tips. With yarn threaded on a tapestry needle, use the Kitchener st (see Techniques) to graft 43 (43, 45, 45) sts from beg of row to the 43 (43, 45, 45) sts at the end of the row—45 (45, 49, 49) sts rem.

Armhole Trim

With WS facing and a new length of yarn, pick up and knit 3 sts over the gap created at the grafting row—48 (48, 52, 52) sts. Arrange sts evenly over 3 dpn, so beg of rnd is after the picked-up sts.

Use a provisional method to CO 3 sts onto a fourth dpn and sl them onto first dpn. Using yarn attached from picking up the sts, k2, ssk, *sl 3 sts from right needle to left needle, k2, ssk; rep from * until only the 3 sts rem. Carefully remove waste yarn from 3 provisional trim sts and place the 3 sts onto an empty dpn. Graft 3 sts from each needle together using Kitchener st.

Carefully remove waste yarn from the provisional body CO sts and place the 131 (131, 139, 139) sts onto cir. Join sides and work armhole trim the same as the other side.

Weave in all ends. Block again if desired.

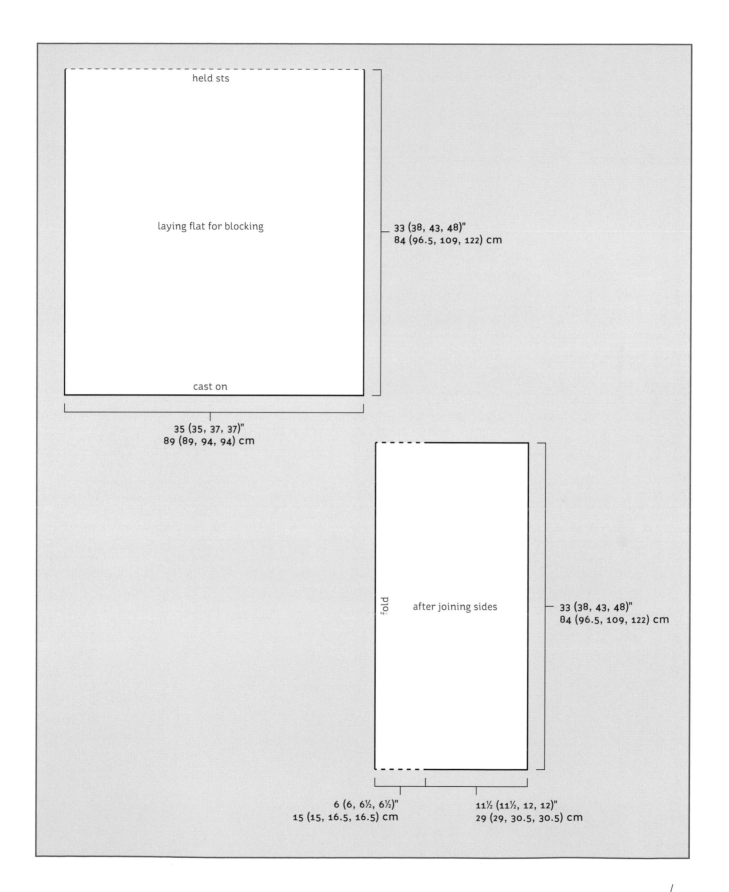

held sts

laying flat for blocking

33 (38, 43, 48)"
84 (96.5, 109, 122) cm

cast on

35 (35, 37, 37)"
89 (89, 94, 94) cm

fold

after joining sides

33 (38, 43, 48)"
84 (96.5, 109, 122) cm

6 (6, 6½, 6½)"
15 (15, 16.5, 16.5) cm

11½ (11½, 12, 12)"
29 (29, 30.5, 30.5) cm

serra TURTLENECK

FINISHED SIZE

About 34¼ (37¼, 40, 42¾, 45¾, 48½)" (87 [94.5, 101.5, 108.5, 116, 123] cm) bust circumference.

Pullover shown measures 37¼" (94.5 cm).

YARN

Worsted weight (#4 medium).

SHOWN HERE: Brooklyn Tweed Shelter (100% wool; 140 yd [128 m]/50 g): #13 Wool Socks, 7 (8, 9, 10, 10, 11) skeins.

NEEDLES

Size U.S. 7 (4.5 mm): 16"(40 cm) and 24" (60 cm) circular (cir), and a set of 4 or 5 double-pointed (dpn).

Adjust needle sizes if necessary to obtain the correct gauge.

NOTIONS

Smooth waste yarn for provisional CO; stitch markers (m): 1 for beg of rnd, 2 for faux seam sts, 7 for yoke shaping; tapestry needle.

GAUGE

17 sts and 28 rnds = 4" (10 cm) in St st worked in the rnd.

This modern minimalist pullover is worked from the top down with decorative faux seam lines. The rustic woolly texture of the yarn juxtaposed with the sleek silhouette echoes the weathered steel sculpture of Richard Serra.

Stitch Guide

APPLIED I-CORD BO: Use a provisional method (see Techniques) to CO 3 sts onto the left needle at the beg of the rnd. *K2, ssk, sl 3 sts from the right needle back onto the left needle and rep from * until all the sts have been worked—3 sts rem. Break yarn, leaving a tail at least 9" (23 cm) for grafting. Carefully remove waste yarn from provisional CO and place 3 sts onto an empty needle. Use the Kitchener St (see Techniques) to graft the live sts together.

NOTES

- The sweater is worked from the top down without seams.
- This project uses 12 markers on the yoke. I recommend color coding them to differentiate the "faux seam" stitch marker from the increase markers and the beginning of round marker.

Yoke

With 16" (40 cm) cir, use a provisional method (see Techniques) to CO 72 (72, 72, 88, 88, 88) sts. Place marker (pm) for beg of rnd and join for working in the rnd, being careful not to twist sts.

Collar

EST FAUX SEAM STITCHES: K26 (26, 26, 32, 32, 32), pm, sl 1 st purlwise with yarn in back (pwise wyb) for "faux seam," k35 (35, 35, 43, 43, 43), pm, sl 1 pwise wyb for faux seam, k9 (9, 9, 11, 11, 11) to end.

RND 1: Knit.

RND 2: *Knit to m, sl m, sl 1 st pwise wyb for faux seam; rep from * once more, knit to end.

Rep the last 2 rnds until piece measures 6" (15 cm) from CO, ending after Rnd 1.

Shape Yoke

NOTE: Change to longer circular needle when sts no longer fit comfortably on 16" [40-cm] cir.

SET-UP RND: [K1, M1, k7 (7, 7, 9, 9, 9), M1, pm] 3 times, k2, sl m, sl 1 st pwise wyb for faux seam, k1, [k1, M1, k7 (7, 7, 9, 9, 9), M1, pm] 4 times, k2, sl m, sl 1 st pwise wyb for faux seam, k2, M1, k7 (7, 7, 9, 9, 9), M1—88 (88, 88, 104, 104, 104) sts.

Work 3 rnds even, maintaining the faux seam st by slipping it on every other rnd.

INC RND: [K1, M1, knit to next inc m, M1, sl m] 3 times, k2, slm, sl 1 st pwise wyb for faux seam, k1, [k1, M1, knit to next inc m, M1, sl m] 4 times, k2, sl m, sl 1 st pwise wyb for faux seam, k2, m1, knit to beg of rnd m, M1—16 sts inc'd.

Rep the last 4 rnds 2 (2, 3, 3, 4, 5) times—136 (136, 152, 168, 184, 200) sts.

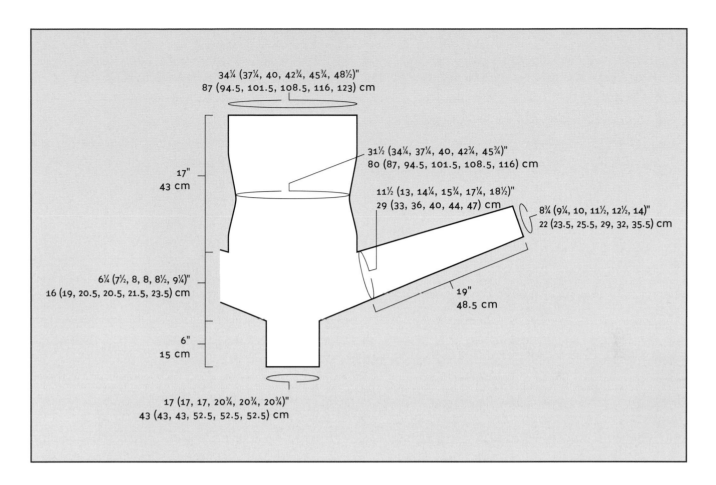

34¼ (37¼, 40, 42¾, 45¾, 48½)"
87 (94.5, 101.5, 108.5, 116, 123) cm

31½ (34¼, 37¼, 40, 42¾, 45¾)"
80 (87, 94.5, 101.5, 108.5, 116) cm

17"
43 cm

11½ (13, 14¼, 15¾, 17¼, 18½)"
29 (33, 36, 40, 44, 47) cm

8¾ (9¼, 10, 11½, 12½, 14)"
22 (23.5, 25.5, 29, 32, 35.5) cm

6¼ (7½, 8, 8, 8½, 9¼)"
16 (19, 20.5, 20.5, 21.5, 23.5) cm

19"
48.5 cm

6"
15 cm

17 (17, 17, 20¾, 20¾, 20¾)"
43 (43, 43, 52.5, 52.5, 52.5) cm

[Work 7 rnds even, maintaining the faux seam sts by slipping them on every other rnd. Rep inc rnd] 2 (3, 3, 3, 3, 3) times—168 (184, 200, 216, 232, 248) sts.

[Work 3 rnds even, maintaining the faux seam sts by slipping them on every other rnd. Rep inc rnd] 3 times—216 (232, 248, 264, 280, 296) sts.

Remove the inc markers and work 3 rnds even, maintaining the faux seam sts by slipping them on every other rnd.

DIVIDE BODY AND SLEEVES: K59 (63, 67, 71, 75, 79) sts for back, BO 42 (46, 50, 54, 58, 62) sts removing the faux seam m, k66 (70, 74, 78, 82, 86) sts for front, BO 42 (46, 50, 54, 58, 62) sts removing the faux seam m, k7 to end—132 (140, 148, 156, 164, 172) sts rem: 66 (70, 74, 78, 82, 86) sts each back and front.

Body

CAST ON FOR UNDERARMS: Remove beg of rnd m, knit to the BO sts, use the backward-loop method (see Techniques) to CO 3 (4, 5, 6, 7, 8) sts, pm for faux seam, CO 4 (5, 6, 7, 8, 9) more sts, knit to the BO sts, use the backward-loop method to CO 3 (4, 5, 6, 7, 8) sts, pm for new beg of rnd, CO 4 (5, 6, 7, 8, 9) sts, knit to end of the rnd—146 (158, 170, 182, 194, 206) sts.

RND 1: Knit.

RND 2: *Sl 1 st pwise wyb for faux seam, knit to next m, sl m; rep from * once more.

Rep the last 2 rnds until piece measures 2" (5 cm) from underarm CO, ending after Rnd 1.

Shape Waist

DEC RND: *Sl 1 st pwise wyb for faux seam, k1, k2tog, knit to 3 sts before next m, ssk, k1, sl m; rep from * once more—4 sts dec'd.

Work 11 rnds even, maintaining the faux seam sts by slipping them on every other rnd.

Rep the last 12 rows 2 times—134 (146, 158, 170, 182, 194) sts.

INC RND: *Sl 1 st pwise wyb for faux seam, k1, M1L (see Techniques), knit to 1 st before next m, M1R (see Techniques), k1, sl m; rep from * once more—4 sts inc'd.

Work 11 rnds even, maintaining the faux seam sts by slipping them on every other rnd.

Rep the last 12 rows 2 times—146 (158, 170, 182, 194, 206) sts.

Cont working even as est, maintaining the faux seam sts by slipping them on every other rnd, until body measures 17" (43 cm) from underarm CO, ending after a knit rnd without slipped faux seam sts.

Work applied I-cord BO (see Stitch Guide).

Sleeve

With dpn and WS facing (so ridge from picked-up sts is on the RS), beg at underarm CO sts, 1 st to the right of the faux seam st, pick up and knit 3 (4, 5, 6, 7, 8) sts along the first half of the underarm CO sts, 42 (46, 50, 54, 58, 62) sts along the BO sts (1 st in each BO st), and 4 (5, 6, 7, 8, 9) sts from the rem CO underarm sts—49 (55, 61, 67, 73, 79) sts.

Wrap the next st and turn so the RS is facing. Pm for beg of rnd and join for working in the rnd.

RND 1: Sl 1 pwise wyb for faux seam, knit to end.

RND 2: Knit.

Rep the last 2 rnds 4 more times.

Shape Sleeve

DEC RND: Sl 1 pwise wyb for faux seam, k1, k2tog, knit to last 3 sts, ssk, k1—2 sts dec'd.

Work 15 (11, 9, 9, 7, 7) rnds even, maintaining the faux seam st by slipping it on every other rnd.

Rep the last 16 (12, 10, 10, 8, 8) rnds 5 (7, 8, 8, 9, 9) times—37 (39, 43, 49, 53, 59) sts rem.

Work even until piece measures 19" (48.5 cm) from the pick up rnd, ending after a knit rnd without slipped faux seam sts.

Work applied I-cord BO.

Work second sleeve the same as the first.

Finishing

Carefully remove waste yarn from provisional CO at neck edge and place 72 (72, 72, 88, 88, 88) sts onto 16" (40 cm) cir. Work applied I-cord BO.

Block to measurements. Weave in ends.

van der zee CLOCHE

FINISHED SIZE
About 21¼" (54 cm) circumference.

YARN
Worsted weight (#4 medium).

SHOWN HERE: Dream in Color Calm
(100% wool: 240 yd [220 m]/100 g):
Shiny Moss, 1 skein.

NEEDLES
Size U.S. 7 (4.5 mm): 16" (40 cm) circular (cir)
and set of 4 or 5 double-pointed (dpn).

*Adjust needle sizes if necessary to obtain
the correct gauge.*

NOTIONS
Stitch marker (m); tapestry needle.

GAUGE
17 sts and 32 rnds = 4" (10 cm) in seed st
worked in rnds.

This flapperesque cloche-style hat is a versatile
pattern to have in your knitting arsenal: leave
it unembellished, and you have the perfect
quick-to-knit gift, a simple beanie for a man
or a woman; add just a few leaves—or a lot—to
suit your taste. Photographer James Van Der
Zee, whose work documented the Harlem
Renaissance, inspires its Jazz Age coolness.

NOTE: *When trimming the hat, refer to the photos, then lay out the leaves before you begin to sew. Group them into clusters of 2 or 3 and play with the arrangement. When you begin to attach them, start at the center back (where the beginning/end of the round is) and choose one direction to work out from until about one-third of the brim is covered.*

Hat

With cir, CO 90 sts.

EST SEED ST AS FOLL:

RND 1: *K1, p1; rep from *.

RND 2: *P1, k1; rep from *.

Rep the last 2 rnds until piece measures 6" (15 cm) from CO.

Shape Crown

NOTE: *Change to dpn when sts no longer fit comfortably on cir.*

DEC RND 1: *Work 6 sts in seed st as est, sl1-k2tog-psso (see Abbreviations), work 12 sts in seed st as est, p3tog, work 6 sts in seed st as est; rep from * 2 times—78 sts rem.

Work 2 rnds in seed st.

DEC RND 2: *Work 5 sts in seed st, sl1-k2tog-psso, work 10 sts in seed st, p3tog, work 5 sts in seed st; rep from * 2 times—66 sts rem.

Work 2 rnds in seed st as est.

DEC RND 3: *Work 4 sts in seed st, sl1-k2tog-psso, work 8 sts in seed st, p3tog, work 4 sts in seed st; rep from * 2 times—54 sts rem.

Work 2 rnds in seed st as est.

DEC RND 4: *Work 3 sts in seed st, sl1-k2tog-psso, work 6 sts in seed st, p3tog, work 3 sts in seed st; rep from * 2 times—42 sts rem.

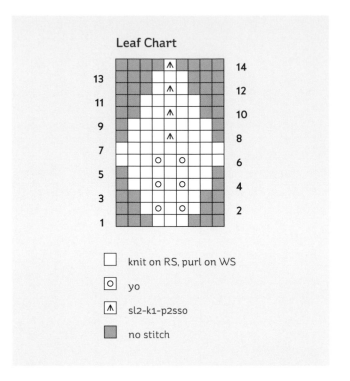

Leaf Chart

☐ knit on RS, purl on WS

⊙ yo

⋏ sl2-k1-p2sso

▓ no stitch

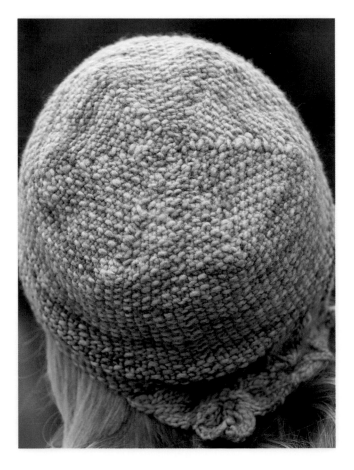

Work 2 rnds in seed st as est.

DEC RND 5: *Work 2 sts in seed st, sl1-k2tog-psso, work 4 sts in seed st, p3tog, work 2 sts in seed st; rep from * 2 times—30 sts rem.

Work 2 rnds in seed st as est.

DEC RND 6: *Work 1 st in seed st, sl1-k2tog-psso, work 2 sts in seed st, p3tog, work 1 st in seed st; rep from * 2 times—18 sts rem.

Work 2 rnds in seed st as est.

DEC RND 7: *Sl1-k2tog-psso, p3tog; rep from * 2 times—6 sts rem.

Break yarn, leaving at least a 9" (23 cm) tail. Thread tail through rem sts and pull tight.

Leaves

(make 12)

With dpn, CO 3 sts. Do not join; work back and forth in rows.

Work Rows 1–14 of Leaf chart—1 st rem.

Break yarn and pull the tail through the rem st.

Finishing

Beg at the center back of hat at the tail from the CO, finish the hat by appliquéing leaves (see Note). Weave in ends. Block as desired.

moses HOODIE

FINISHED SIZE

About 32¾ (36, 39¼, 42½, 45¾, 48¾)" (83 [91.5, 99.5, 108, 116, 124] cm) bust circumference, closed.

YARN

DK weight (#3 light).

SHOWN HERE: Green Mountain Spinnery New Mexico Organic (100% wool; 180 yd [165 m]/57 g): Grey, 8 (8, 9, 10, 10, 11) skeins.

NEEDLES

BODY—Size U.S. 6 (4 mm): straight, 24" (60 cm) circular (cir), and set of 4 or 5 double-pointed (dpn).

EDGING—Size U.S. 4 (3.5 mm): 24" (60 cm) cir and set of 4 or 5 dpn.

Adjust needle sizes if necessary to obtain the correct gauge.

NOTIONS

Stitch markers (m); stitch holders or waste yarn; tapestry needle; 20" (51 cm) separating zipper and sewing thread to match, hand-sewing needle for zipper.

GAUGE

20 sts and 29 rows = 4" (10 cm) in St st on larger needles.

Scandinavian textured knitting, and the homespun texture of the Green Mountain Spinnery yarn, give this hooded sweatshirt an unfussy sweetness, like the painitings of Anna Mary Robertson Moses—also known as Grandma Moses. The hoodie has gone from an item of gym clothing to an icon of casual American dress.

This piece of Americana is worked from the bottom up with roomy kangaroo pockets and sewn-in sleeves.

NOTE: *Circular needles are used to accommodate a large number of stitches. Do not join; work back and forth in rows.*

Pocket Linings
Left Pocket Lining

With larger needles, CO 31 sts. Beg with a WS row, work 5 rows even in St st (knit on RS, purl on WS), ending after a WS row.

Place sts onto st holder or waste yarn. Break yarn.

Right Pocket Lining

With larger needles, CO 31 sts. Beg with a RS row, work 5 rows even in St st, ending after a RS row.

Place sts onto st holder or waste yarn. Break yarn.

Body

With smaller cir, CO 163 (179, 195, 211, 227, 243) sts. Do not join; work back and forth in rows.

EST RIB (WS): P1, *k1, p1: rep from *.

Work in 1×1 rib as est until piece measures 2¼" (5.5 cm) from beg, ending after a WS row.

Purl 1 WS row.

Change to larger cir.

PLACE MARKERS FOR SIDES (RS): K41 (45, 49, 53, 57, 61) sts for right front, place marker (pm), k81 (89, 97, 105, 113, 121) sts for back, pm, k41 (45, 49, 53, 57, 61) sts for left front.

Work 5 rows even St st (knit on RS, purl on WS), ending after a WS row.

Pocket Linings and Body

DIVIDE POCKETS FROM BODY (RS): K33, place those 33 sts onto a st holder or waste yarn for right pocket, knit to last 33 sts, place rem unworked 33 sts onto a st holder or waste yarn for left pocket, place 31 held sts from left pocket lining (with RS facing) onto the left needle and knit to end—128 (144, 160, 176, 192, 208) sts.

NEXT ROW (WS): Purl to end, place 31 sts from right pocket lining onto the left needle (with WS facing), and purl to end—159 (175, 191, 207, 223, 239) sts.

Work 2 rows even in St st, ending after a WS row.

Shape Waist

DEC ROW (RS): Knit to 2 sts before m, ssk, sl m, k1, k2tog, knit to 3 sts before m, ssk, k1, sl m, k2tog, knit to end—4 sts dec'd.

Work 11 rows even.

Rep the last 12 rows 2 times—147 (163, 179, 195, 211, 227) sts.

NEXT ROW (RS): BO 31 sts for right pocket lining, knit to end—116 (132, 148, 164, 180, 196) sts rem.

Body Chart

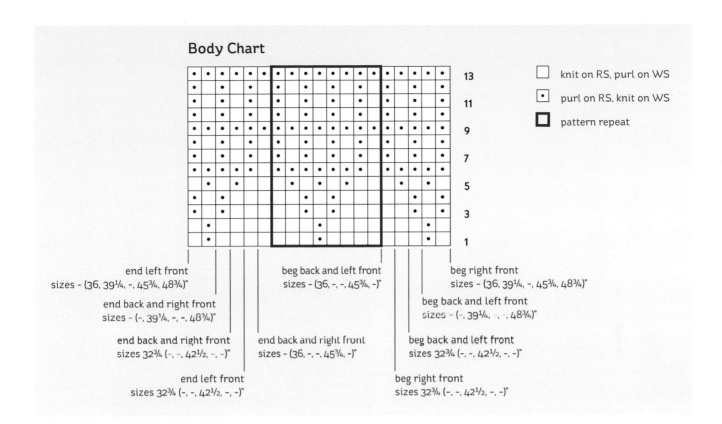

	knit on RS, purl on WS			
	purl on RS, knit on WS			
	pattern repeat			

end left front
sizes - (36, 39¼, -, 45¾, 48¾)"

end back and right front
sizes - (-, 39¼, -, -, 48¾)"

end back and right front
sizes 32¾ (-, -, 42½, -, -)"

end left front
sizes 32¾ (-, -, 42½, -, -)"

beg back and left front
sizes - (36, -, -, 45¾, -)"

end back and right front
sizes - (36, -, -, 45¾, -)"

beg right front
sizes - (36, 39¼, -, 45¾, 48¾)"

beg back and left front
sizes - (-, 39¼, -, -, 48¾)"

beg back and left front
sizes 32¾ (-, -, 42½, -, -)"

beg right front
sizes 32¾ (-, -, 42½, -, -)"

NEXT ROW (WS): BO 31 sts for left pocket lining, purl to end—85 (101, 117, 133, 149, 165) sts rem. Keep sts on cir and set aside. Break yarn.

Left Front Pocket

Return 33 held left front pocket sts to larger straight needle and rejoin yarn, preparing to work a RS row.

Work 40 rows even in St st, ending after a WS row. Place sts onto the left front end of cir needle with body sts. Break yarn.

Right Front Pocket

Return 33 held right front pocket sts to larger straight needle and rejoin yarn, preparing to work a WS row. Work 39 rows even in St st, ending after a WS row. Place sts onto the right front end of cir needle with body and left front pocket sts.

Rejoin Pockets and Body

DEC ROW (RS): With larger cir, k33 right pocket sts, knit body sts to 2 sts before m, ssk, sl m, k1, k2tog, knit to 3 sts before next m, ssk, k1, sl m, k2tog, knit to end of body sts, k33 left pocket sts—147 (163, 179, 195, 211, 227) sts.

Work 11 rows even, ending after a WS row.

INC ROW (RS): Knit to m, M1R (see Techniques), sl m, k1, M1L (see Techniques), knit to 1 st before m, M1R, k1, sl m, M1L, knit to end—4 sts inc'd.

Rep the last 12 rows once more—155 (171, 187, 203, 219, 235) sts.

[Work 7 rows even, then rep inc row] 2 times—163 (179, 195, 211, 227, 243) sts.

Work even in St st until piece measures 16" (40.5 cm) from beg, ending after a WS row.

Divide Back and Fronts

NEXT ROW (RS): K37 (40, 43, 46, 49, 52) sts for right front, BO next 7 (9, 11, 13, 15, 17) sts, removing m, k75 (81, 87, 93, 99, 105) sts for back, BO next 7 (9, 11, 13, 15, 17) sts, removing m, knit rem 37 (40, 43, 46, 49, 52) sts for left front.

Continue working back and forth on left front sts only. Place sts for the right front and back onto st holders or waste yarn.

Left Front

Shape Armhole

Purl 1 WS row.

DEC ROW (RS): K1, k2tog, knit to end—1 st dec'd.

Rep the last 2 rows 4 (5, 5, 5, 6, 6) times—32 (34, 37, 40, 42, 45) sts rem.

Work even in St st until armhole measures 5¼ (5½, 5¾, 6, 6¼, 6½)" (13.5 [14, 14.5, 15, 16, 16.5] cm) from divide, ending after a RS row.

Shape Neck

NEXT ROW (WS): BO 8 sts, work in patt to end—24 (26, 29, 32, 34, 37) sts rem.

EST PATT (RS): Work 2 sts in St st, beg and end where indicated for your size, work 20 (22, 25, 28, 30, 33) sts in Body chart, work last 2 sts in St st (keep first and last 2 sts in St st throughout).

NEXT ROW (WS): BO 4 sts, work in patt to end—20 (22, 25, 28, 30, 33) sts rem.

Work 1 RS row even.

NEXT ROW (WS): BO 3 (3, 3, 4, 4, 4) sts, work in patt to end—17 (19, 22, 24, 26, 29) sts rem.

Work 1 RS row even.

NEXT ROW (WS): BO 2 (2, 2, 2, 2, 3) sts, work in patt to end—15 (17, 20, 22, 24, 26) sts rem.

Work 1 RS row even.

NEXT ROW (WS): BO 1 sts, work in patt to end—1 st dec'd.

Rep the last 2 rows 0 (1, 2, 2, 2, 2) times—14 (15, 17, 19, 21, 23) sts rem.

Cont working as est until RS Row 13 of patt is completed. Armhole should measure 7¼ (7½, 7¾, 8, 8¼, 8½)" (18.5 [19, 19.5, 20.5, 21, 21.5] cm).

Shape Shoulder with Short-Rows

SHORT-ROW 1 (WS): Purl to last 5 (5, 5, 6, 7, 7) sts, wrap next st, and turn so RS is facing.

Purl 1 RS row.

SHORT-ROW 2 (WS): Purl to last 10 (10, 11, 12, 14, 15) sts, wrap next st, and turn so RS is facing.

Purl 1 RS row.

NEXT ROW (WS): Purl to end, picking up the wraps and working them tog with the sts they wrap as they appear. Place sts onto st holder or waste yarn. Break yarn.

Back

Return 75 (81, 87, 93, 99, 105) held back sts to larger needle and join yarn, preparing to work a WS row.

Shape Armholes

Purl 1 WS row.

DEC ROW (RS): K1, k2tog, knit to last 3 sts, ssk, k1—2 sts dec'd.

Rep the last 2 rows 4 (5, 5, 5, 6, 6) times—65 (69, 75, 81, 85, 91) sts rem.

Cont working even in St st until armholes measure 5¼ (5½, 5¾, 6, 6¼, 6½)" (13.5 [14, 14.5, 15, 16, 16.5] cm) from divide, ending after a WS row.

EST PATT (RS): Work 2 sts in St st, beg and end where indicated for your size, work 61 (65, 71, 77, 81, 87) sts in Body chart, work 2 sts in St st.

Cont working as est until RS Row 13 of patt is completed. Armhole should measure 7¼ (7½, 7¾, 8, 8¼, 8½)" (18.5 [19, 19.5, 20.5, 21, 21.5] cm).

Shape Shoulders with Short-Rows

SHORT-ROW 1 (WS): Purl to last 5 (5, 5, 6, 7, 7) sts, wrap next st, and turn so RS is facing; (RS) purl to last 5 (5, 5, 6, 7, 7) sts, wrap next st, and turn so WS is facing.

SHORT-ROW 2 (WS): Purl to last 10 (10, 11, 12, 14, 15) sts, wrap next st, and turn so RS is facing; (RS) purl to last 10 (10, 11, 12, 14, 15) sts, wrap next st and turn so WS is facing.

NEXT 2 ROWS: Purl to end, picking up the wraps and working them tog with the sts they wrap as they appear.

Place all sts onto st holder or waste yarn. Break yarn.

Right Front

Return 37 (40, 43, 46, 49, 52) held right front sts to larger needle and join yarn, preparing to work a WS row.

Shape Armhole

Purl 1 WS row.

DEC ROW (RS): Knit to last 3 sts, ssk, k1—1 st dec'd.

Rep the last 2 rows 4 (5, 5, 5, 6, 6) times—32 (34, 37, 40, 42, 45) sts rem.

Work even in St st until armhole measures 5¼ (5½, 5¾, 6, 6¼, 6½)" (13.5 [14, 14.5, 15, 16, 16.5] cm) from divide, ending after a WS row.

Shape Neck

BO AND EST PATT (RS): BO 8 sts, work 2 sts in St st, beg and end where indicated for your size, work 20 (22, 25, 28, 30, 33) sts in Body chart, work last 2 sts in St st (keep first and last 2 sts in St st throughout).

Work 1 WS row even.

NEXT ROW (RS): BO 4 sts, work in patt to end—20 (22, 25, 28, 30, 33) sts rem.

Work 1 WS row even.

NEXT ROW (RS): BO 3 (3, 3, 4, 4, 4) sts, work in patt to end—17 (19, 22, 24, 26, 29) sts rem.

Work 1 WS row even.

NEXT ROW (RS): BO 2 (2, 2, 2, 2, 3) sts, work in patt to end—15 (17, 20, 22, 24, 26) sts rem.

Work 1 WS row even.

NEXT ROW (RS): BO 1 sts, work in patt to end—1 st dec'd.

Rep the last 2 rows 0 (1, 2, 2, 2, 2) times—14 (15, 17, 19, 21, 23) sts rem.

Cont working as est until RS Row 13 of patt is completed.

Purl 1 WS row. Armhole should measure 7¼ (7½, 7¾, 8, 8¼, 8½)" (18.5 [19, 19.5, 20.5, 21, 21.5] cm).

Shape Shoulder with Short-Rows

SHORT-ROW 1 (RS): Purl to last 5 (5, 5, 6, 7, 7) sts, wrap next st, and turn so WS is facing.

Purl 1 WS row.

SHORT-ROW 2 (RS): Purl to last 10 (10, 11, 12, 14, 15) sts, wrap next st, and turn so WS is facing.

Purl 1 WS row.

NEXT ROW (RS): Purl to end, picking up the wraps and working them tog with the sts they wrap as they appear. Place sts onto st holder or waste yarn. Break yarn.

Sleeve

With smaller needles, CO 40 (40, 48, 48, 56, 56) sts. Divide sts evenly over 3 or 4 dpn. Pm for beg of rnd and join for working in the rnd, being careful not to twist sts.

EST RIB: *K1, p1; rep from *.

Work in 1×1 rib as est until piece measures 2½" (6.5 cm) from beg.

Work Rnds 1–27 of Sleeve chart.

Change to larger needles.

Shape Sleeve

INC RND: K1, M1L, knit to end, M1R–2 sts inc'd.

Knit 9 (7, 9, 7, 7, 6) rnds even.

Rep the last 10 (8, 10, 8, 8, 7) rnds 7 (9, 8, 10, 9, 11) times–56 (60, 66, 70, 76, 80) sts.

Cont working even in St st (knit every rnd) until piece measures 19" (48.5 cm) from beg, ending 3 (4, 5, 6, 7, 8) sts before the beg of rnd m.

Sleeve Chart

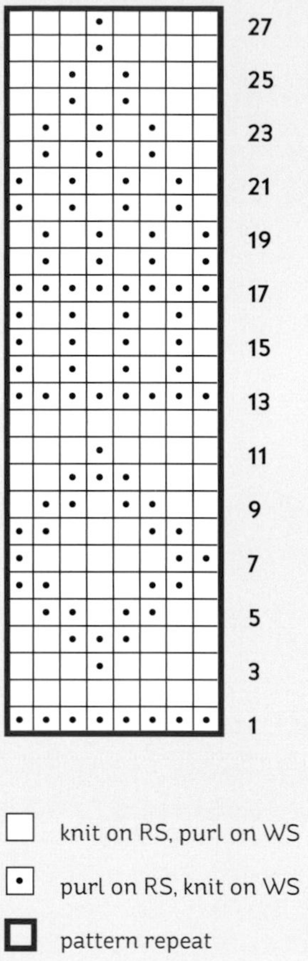

Sleeve chart with 27 rows (odd numbers 1–27 labeled on right side)

- ☐ knit on RS, purl on WS
- ☒ purl on RS, knit on WS
- ☐ pattern repeat

Shape Cap

NEXT RND: BO next 7 (9, 11, 13, 15, 17) sts, knit to end–49 (51, 55, 57, 61, 63) sts rem.

Cont working back and forth in rows.

Purl 1 WS row.

DEC ROW (RS): K1, k2tog, knit to last 3 sts, ssk, k1–2 sts dec'd.

Rep the last 2 rows 4 (5, 5, 5, 15, 16) times–39 (39, 43, 45, 29, 29) sts rem.

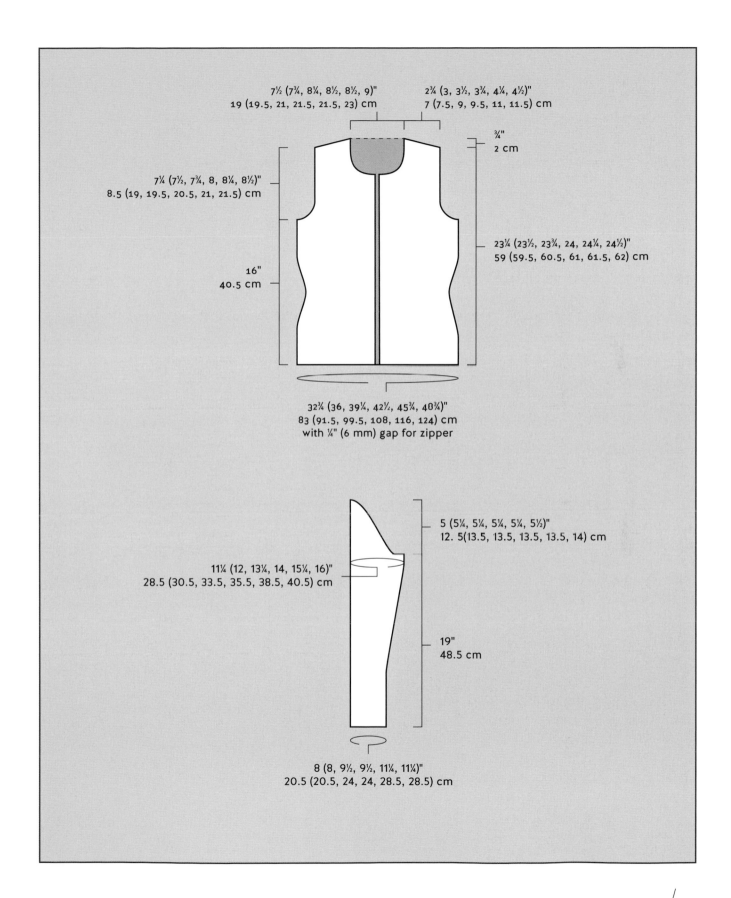

7½ (7¾, 8¼, 8½, 8½, 9)"
19 (19.5, 21, 21.5, 21.5, 23) cm

2¾ (3, 3½, 3¾, 4¼, 4½)"
7 (7.5, 9, 9.5, 11, 11.5) cm

¾"
2 cm

7¼ (7½, 7¾, 8, 8¼, 8½)"
8.5 (19, 19.5, 20.5, 21, 21.5) cm

23¼ (23½, 23¾, 24, 24¼, 24½)"
59 (59.5, 60.5, 61, 61.5, 62) cm

16"
40.5 cm

32¾ (36, 39¼, 42½, 45¾, 40¾)"
83 (91.5, 99.5, 108, 116, 124) cm
with ¼" (6 mm) gap for zipper

5 (5¼, 5¼, 5¼, 5¼, 5½)"
12. 5(13.5, 13.5, 13.5, 13.5, 14) cm

11¼ (12, 13¼, 14, 15¼, 16)"
28.5 (30.5, 33.5, 35.5, 38.5, 40.5) cm

19"
48.5 cm

8 (8, 9½, 9½, 11¼, 11¼)"
20.5 (20.5, 24, 24, 28.5, 28.5) cm

Sizes 32¾ (36, 39¼, 42½)" only

[Work 3 rnds even, then rep dec row] 3 (3, 2, 1) times—33 (33, 39, 43) sts rem.

[Purl 1 WS row, then rep dec row] 4 (4, 6, 8) times—25 (25, 27, 27) sts rem.

All Sizes:

DEC ROW (WS): P1, ssp, purl to last 3 sts, p2tog, p1—2 sts dec'd.

Rep dec row on RS.

Rep the last 2 rows 2 times—13 (13, 15, 15, 17, 17) sts rem.

BO rem sts.

Make a second sleeve the same as the first.

Finishing

Block pieces to measurements.

Join Shoulders

Return 14 (15, 17, 19, 21, 23) held sts from left front and back shoulders onto larger needle and, with RS facing each other, WS facing out, join the back and front shoulders together using the three-needle BO (see Techniques). Rep for right front and back shoulder, keeping 37 (39, 41, 43, 43, 45) center back sts on holder. Set in sleeves, easing the cap into place.

Hood

With larger cir and RS facing, beg at right front neck edge, pick up and knit 32 (32, 33, 34, 36, 36) sts along right front, return 37 (39, 41, 43, 43, 45) held back sts to empty end of needle and knit across, pick up and knit 32 (32, 33, 34, 36, 36) sts along left front neck edge—101 (103, 107, 111, 115, 117) sts.

Work even in St st until hood measures 12" (30.5 cm) from pick-up row, ending after a RS row.

DIVIDE ROW (WS): P49 (50, 52, 54, 56, 58) sts, p2tog—50 (51, 53, 55, 57, 59) sts rem on each needle. With WS facing together and RS facing out, use Kitchener st (see Techniques) to graft live sts together.

Applied I-cord

With smaller dpn, CO 3 sts. Beg at lower edge of right front, pick up and knit 1 st—4 sts. Slide sts onto right-hand end of dpn, *k3, ssk, pick up and knit 1 st from selvedge; rep from * along right front, around hood and down left front skipping every 3rd or 4th selvedge row.

BO all sts.

Pocket Edging

Sew the pocket linings to the WS of the body.

With smaller needles and RS facing, pick up and knit 29 sts along the pocket opening.

EST RIB (WS): P1, *k1, p1; rep from *.

NEXT ROW (RS): K1, *p1, k1; rep from *.

Rep the last 2 rows 2 times.

BO all sts in rib.

With yarn threaded in a tapestry needle, sew ends of pocket edging to body.

Work second pocket edging the same as the first.

Zipper

Baste the front bands to the zipper tape, easing to fit. Sew zipper to WS using sewing thread and needle. (See Techniques for more information about sewing zippers.)

The zipper can be replaced with a button closer by replacing the I-cord front bands with a 1×1 rib. Mark placement for buttons on the left front and buttonholes on the right front before picking up an odd number of stitches (1×1 rib is a multiple of 2 + 1 stitches).

Weave in all ends. Block again if desired.

sargent PULLOVER

FINISHED SIZE
About 31 (33½, 36¼, 38¾, 41¼)" (79 [85, 92, 98.5, 105] cm) bust circumference.

Pullover shown measures 33½ (85 cm).

YARN
Sportweight (#2 fine).

SHOWN HERE: Rowan Felted Tweed DK (50% merino, 25% alpaca, 25% viscose; 191 yd [175 m]/50 g): #157 camel (MC), 5 (6, 6, 7, 7) skeins; #154 ginger (CC1) and #145 treacle (CC2), 1 (2, 2, 2, 2) skein(s) each; #177 clay (CC3), 1 skein.

NEEDLES
BODY—Size U.S. 5 (3.75 mm): 24" (60 cm) circular (cir) and set of 4 or 5 double-pointed (dpn).

RIBBING—Size U.S 3 (3.25 mm): 16" (40 cm) and 24" (60 cm) cir and set of 4 or 5 dpn.

Adjust needle sizes if necessary to obtain the correct gauge.

NOTIONS
Stitch markers (m); stitch holders or waste yarn; tapestry needle.

GAUGE
25 sts and 25 rnds = 4" (10 cm) in Fair Isle St st, worked in rnds, on larger needles.

24 sts and 28 rnds = 4" (10 cm) in St st, worked in rnds, on larger needles.

The palette for this colorwork pullover was inspired by my grandmother's favorite painter, John Singer Sargent, in his 1920 watercolor portrait of Isabella Stewart Gardner.
The heathery tweeds give depth to the simple 4-stitch motif, and the sewn-in raglan sleeves worked in a single color are a modern twist on a traditional style.

Stitch Guide

1×1 Rib (multiple of 2 sts)

RND 1: *K1, p1; rep from *.

Rep Rnd 1 for patt.

NOTE: *To keep the selvedge edges of the raglans neat for seaming, work the first and last 2 stitches of every row in MC when working the raglan shaping.*

Left Sleeve

With CC2 and smaller needle, CO 48 (52, 54, 56, 60) sts. Divide sts evenly over 3 or 4 dpn, place marker (pm), and join for working in the rnd, being careful not to twist sts. Break CC2 and join MC. Cont working sleeve in MC throughout.

Work in 1×1 rib (see Stitch Guide) until piece measures 2¼" (5.5 cm) from beg.

Change to larger dpn.

Work even in St st (knit all sts, every rnd) until piece measures 4" (10 cm) from beg.

Shape Sleeve

INC RND: K1, M1L (see Techniques), knit to last st, M1R (see Techniques), k1–2 sts inc'd.

Knit 11 (9, 7, 7, 5) rnds even.

Rep the last 12 (10, 8, 8, 6) rnds 7 (8, 10, 12, 13) times—64 (70, 76, 82, 88) sts.

Work even in St st until piece measures 19" (48.5 cm) from beg, ending last rnd 5 (6, 7, 8, 9) sts before the beg of rnd m.

Shape Cap

NEXT ROW (RS): BO 10 (12, 14, 16, 18) sts, knit to end—54 (58, 62, 66, 70) sts rem.

Cont working back and forth in rows.

Purl 1 WS row.

DEC ROW (RS): K2, k2tog, knit to last 4 sts, ssk, k2—2 sts dec'd.

Rep the last 2 rows 4 (6, 8, 9, 11) times—44 (44, 44, 46, 46) sts rem.

[Work 3 rows even in St st, then rep dec row] 4 (3, 3, 2, 1) times—36 (38, 38, 42, 44) sts rem.

[Purl 1 WS row, then rep dec row] 12 (14, 14, 16, 18) times—12 (10, 10, 10, 8) sts rem.

Top of Left Sleeve Cap

NEXT ROW (WS): BO 6 (5, 5, 5, 3) sts, work to end—6 (5, 5, 5, 5) sts rem.

NEXT ROW (RS): K2, k2tog, knit to end—5 (4, 4, 4, 4) sts rem. BO rem sts.

Right Seeve

Work the same as the left sleeve, ending before top of left sleeve cap.

Color Chart

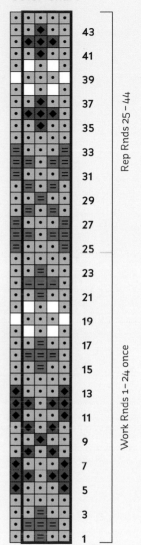

Rep Rnds 25–44

Work Rnds 1–24 once

43
41
39
37
35
33
31
29
27
25
23
21
19
17
15
13
11
9
7
5
3
1

- □ with MC knit on RS, purl on WS
- ▤ with CC1 knit on RS, purl on WS
- ◆ with CC2 knit on RS, purl on WS
- □ with CC3 knit on RS, purl on WS
- □ pattern repeat

Top of Right Sleeve Cap

Purl 1 WS row.

NEXT ROW (RS): BO 6 (5, 5, 5, 3) sts, knit to last 4 sts, ssk, k2–5 (4, 4, 4, 4) sts rem. BO rem sts.

Body

With CC2 and smaller 24" (60 cm) cir, CO 194 (210, 226, 242, 258) sts. Pm and join for working in the rnd, being careful not to twist sts. Break CC2 and join MC.

Work in 1×1 rib until piece measures 1¾" (4.5 cm) from beg.

Change to larger cir.

NEXT RND: With MC, k97 (105, 113, 121, 129) sts, pm for side, k97 (105, 113, 121, 129) sts to end.

EST PATT: Join CC1 and *work the 4-st red rep box of Color chart 24 (26, 28, 30, 32) times, then work the last st of Color chart to m, sl m; rep from * once more.

Cont working Color chart as est until Rnd 24 is completed, then rep Rnds 25–44; *and at the same time*, when piece measures 4" (10 cm) from beg, shape waist as foll:

Shape Waist

DEC RND: *K1, k2tog, work as est to 3 sts before m, ssk, k1, sl m; rep from * once more—4 sts dec'd.

Work 9 rnds even.

Rep the last 10 rnds 2 times—182 (198, 214, 230, 246) sts rem.

Work 2 rnds even.

INC RND: *K1, M1L, work as est to 1 st before m, M1R, k1, sl m; rep from * once more—4 sts inc'd.

Work 9 rnds even.

Rep the last 12 rnds 2 times—194 (210, 226, 242, 258) sts.

Work even as est until piece measures 14½" (37 cm), ending last rnd 5 (6, 7, 8, 9) sts before the beg of rnd m.

Divide Back and Front

NEXT RND: BO 10 (12, 14, 16, 18) sts, removing m, work front sts as est to 5 (6, 7, 8, 9) sts before next m, BO 10 (12, 14, 16, 18) sts, removing m, work to end for back—87 (93, 99, 105, 111) sts rem for each back and front. Cont working back and forth in rows on back sts only. Place front sts onto st holder or waste yarn.

Back
Shape Raglan

Work 1 WS row even.

DEC ROW (RS): K2, k2tog, work as est to last 4 sts, ssk, k2—2 sts dec'd.

Rep the last 2 rows 8 (8, 10, 11, 12) times—69 (75, 77, 81, 85) sts rem.

Work 3 rows even.

Rep dec row—67 (73, 75, 79, 83) sts rem.

[Work 1 WS row even, then rep dec row] 12 (14, 14, 14, 14) times—43 (45, 47, 51, 55) sts rem.

Work 1 WS row even. BO all sts.

Front

Return 87 (93, 99, 105, 111) held front sts to larger needle and join yarn, preparing to work a WS row.

Shape Raglan

Work 1 WS row even.

DEC ROW (RS): K2, k2tog, work as est to last 4 sts, ssk, k2—2 sts dec'd.

Rep the last 2 rows 4 (7, 10, 10, 14) times—77 (77, 77, 83, 81) sts rem.

[Work 3 rows even, then rep dec row] 3 (2, 2, 2, 1) times—71 (73, 73, 79, 79) sts rem.

Work 1 WS row even.

Shape Neck

NEXT ROW (RS): Work 31 sts for left front, BO the next 9 (11, 11, 17, 17) sts, work to end for right front. Cont working back and forth on right front sts, placing left front sts onto st holder or waste yarn.

Right Front

Work 1 WS row even.

Shape Neck and Raglan

DEC ROW (RS): BO 2 sts, work as est to last 4 sts, ssk, k2—3 sts dec'd.

Work 1 WS row even.

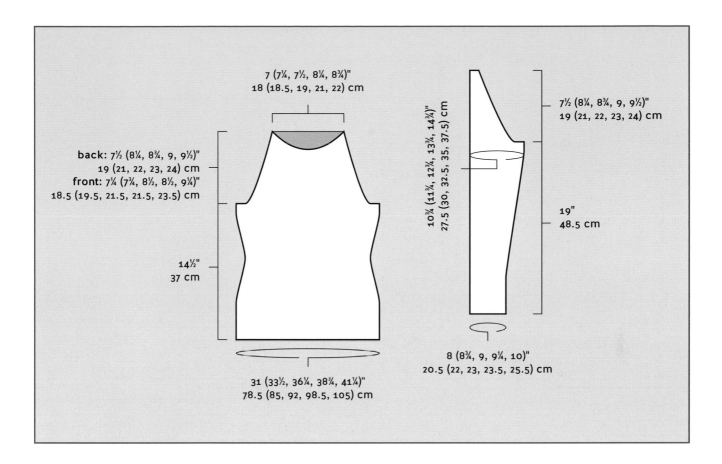

7 (7¼, 7½, 8¼, 8¾)"
18 (18.5, 19, 21, 22) cm

back: 7½ (8¼, 8¾, 9, 9½)"
19 (21, 22, 23, 24) cm
front: 7¼ (7¾, 8½, 8½, 9¼)"
18.5 (19.5, 21.5, 21.5, 23.5) cm

14½"
37 cm

31 (33½, 36¼, 38¾, 41¼)"
78.5 (85, 92, 98.5, 105) cm

10¾ (11¾, 12¾, 13¾, 14¾)"
27.5 (30, 32.5, 35, 37.5) cm

7½ (8¼, 8¾, 9, 9½)"
19 (21, 22, 23, 24) cm

19"
48.5 cm

8 (8¾, 9, 9¼, 10)"
20.5 (22, 23, 23.5, 25.5) cm

Rep the last 2 rows 8 times—4 sts rem.

DEC ROW (RS): BO 1 st, ssk, then bring first st on right needle over the second to BO the last st—1 st rem.

Fasten off.

Left Front

Return 31 held left front sts to larger needle and join yarn, preparing to work a WS row.

Work 1 WS row even.

Shape Neck and Raglan

DEC ROW (RS): K2, k2tog, work to the end of the row—1 st dec'd.

NEXT ROW: BO 2 sts, work to end—2 sts dec'd.

Rep the last 2 rows 9 times—1 st rem.

Fasten off.

Finishing

Block pieces to measurements.

With MC threaded on a tapestry needle, sew sleeves to body along the raglan.

Neckband

With MC, and 16" (40 cm) cir, beg at the back left shoulder, pick up and knit 98 (100, 102, 112, 116) sts evenly around neck edge. Pm for beg of rnd and join for working in the rnd. Work 1×1 rib for 5 rnds. Break MC yarn and join CC2. BO all sts loosely in rib.

Weave in all ends. Block again if desired.

nevelson
LACE PULLOVER

FINISHED SIZE
About 36¾ (39¾, 42½, 45½, 48¼)" (93.5 [101, 108, 115.5, 122.5] cm) bust circumference.

Pullover shown measures 39¾" (101 cm).

YARN
Sportweight (#2 fine).

SHOWN HERE: Lorna's Laces Shepherd Sport (100% superwash merino wool; 200 yd [183 m]/56 g): Patina, 7 (7, 8, 8, 9) skeins.

NEEDLES
BODY—Size U.S. 4 (3.5 mm): 24" (60 cm) circular (cir) and set of 4 or 5 double-pointed (dpn).

RIBBING—Size U.S. 2 (3 mm): 16" (40 cm) and 24" (60 cm) cir and set of 4 or 5 dpn.

Adjust needle sizes if necessary to obtain the correct gauge.

NOTIONS
Stitch markers (m); stitch holders or waste yarn; tapestry needle.

GAUGE
22 sts and 30 rnds = 4" (10 cm) in Lace chart, worked in rnds, on larger needles.

25 sts and 26 rnds = 4" (10 cm) in St st, worked in rnds, on larger needles.

The hand-dyed yarn from Lorna's Laces gives an additional layer of depth to this lace pullover, its texture reminiscent of a Louise Nevelson assemblage. The allover pattern on the body is balanced with three-quarter-length set-in sleeves worked in stockinette stitch.

Stitch Guide

Twisted 1×1 Rib (multiple of 2 sts)

RND 1: *K1tbl, p1tbl; rep from *.

Rep Rnd 1 for patt.

NOTES

- When establishing the Lace chart, work the first stitch of the chart, then repeat the 4 stitches in the red box for the indicated number of repeats, then work the final 4 stitches to the marker; work the second half of the body in the same manner.

- When shaping armholes, be careful to keep the stitch count accurate by working corresponding increase and decrease together. If there are not enough stitches to work both the increase and decrease, work them both in St st (knit on RS, purl on WS) instead. If only 1 yarnover is worked for the sl1-k2tog-psso stitch, work k2tog or ssk instead.

Body

With smaller 24" (60 cm) cir, CO 202 (218, 234, 250, 266) sts. Place marker (pm) for beg of rnd and join for working in the rnd, being careful not to twist sts.

Work in twisted 1×1 rib until piece measures 1" (2.5 cm) from beg.

Change to larger cir.

PLACE MARKER FOR SIDE: K101 (109, 117, 125, 133) sts, pm for side, k101 (109, 117, 125, 133) sts to end.

EST PATT: *Work Lace chart to side m, working the 4-st red rep box 24 (26, 28, 30, 32) times, sl m; rep from * once more (see Notes).

Cont working Lace chart even as est until piece measures 16" (40.5 cm) from beg, ending last rnd 5 (6, 7, 8, 9) sts before beg of the rnd m.

Lace Chart

- ☐ knit on RS, purl on WS
- ⊡ purl on RS, knit on WS
- ◯ yo
- ╱ k2tog
- ╲ ssk
- ⋏ sl1-k2tog-psso
- ☐ pattern repeat

Divide for Back and Front

NEXT RND: BO next 10 (12, 14, 16, 18) sts, removing m, work front sts to 5 (6, 7, 8, 9) sts before m, BO next 10 (12, 14, 16, 18) sts, removing m, work back sts to end—91 (97, 103, 109, 115) sts rem for each back and front. Cont working back and forth on back sts only. Place sts for front onto st holder or waste yarn.

Back

Shape Armholes

Work 1 WS row even.

DEC ROW (RS): K2, k2tog, work to last 4 sts, ssk, k2—2 sts dec'd.

Rep the last 2 rows 4 (5, 6, 7, 8) times—81 (85, 89, 93, 97) sts rem.

Work even as est until armholes measure 7¾ (8, 8½, 8¾, 9)" (19.5 [20.5, 21.5, 22, 23] cm) from divide, ending after a WS row.

Shape Neck

NEXT ROW (RS): Work 16 (18, 18, 20, 20) sts, then place these sts onto a st holder or waste yarn for shoulder, BO 49 (49, 53, 53, 57) sts, work rem 16 (18, 18, 20, 20) sts to end, then place them onto st holder or waste yarn for shoulder. Break yarn.

Front

Return 91 (97, 103, 109, 115) held front sts to larger needle and join yarn, preparing to work a WS row.

Shape Armholes

Work 1 WS row even.

DEC ROW (RS): K2, k2tog, work to last 4 sts, ssk, k2—2 sts dec'd.

Rep the last 2 rows 4 (5, 6, 7, 8) times—81 (85, 89, 93, 97) sts rem.

Work even as est until armholes measure 5¾ (6, 6½, 6¾, 7)" (14.5 [15, 16.5, 17, 18] cm) from divide, ending after a WS row.

Shape Neck

NEXT ROW (RS): Work 36 (38, 40, 42, 44) sts as est for left front, BO the next 9 sts, work to end for right front—36 (38, 40, 42, 44) sts rem on each side. Cont working back and forth on right front sts only. Place sts for left front onto st holder or waste yarn.

Right Front

Work 1 WS row.

NEXT ROW (RS): BO 8 sts, work to end—28 (30, 32, 34, 36) sts rem.

Work 1 WS row.

NEXT ROW (RS): BO 4 sts, work to end—4 sts dec'd.

Rep the last 2 rows 1 (1, 1, 1, 2) times—20 (22, 24, 26, 24) sts rem.

Work 1 WS row.

NEXT ROW (RS): BO 2 sts, work to end—2 sts dec'd.

Rep the last 2 rows 1 (1, 2, 2, 1) times—16 (18, 18, 20, 20) sts rem.

Cont working even as est until armhole measures 7¾ (8, 8½, 8¾, 9)" (19.5 [20.5, 21.5, 22, 23] cm) from divide, ending after a WS row.

Place all sts onto st holders or waste yarn. Break yarn, leaving a tail at least 1 yd (91.5 cm) long.

Left Front

Return 36 (38, 40, 42, 44) held left front sts to larger needle and join yarn, preparing to work a WS row.

NEXT ROW (WS): BO 8 sts, work to end—28 (30, 32, 34, 36) sts rem.

Work 1 RS row.

NEXT ROW (WS): BO 4 sts, work to end—4 sts dec'd.

Work 1 RS row.

Rep the last 2 rows 1 (1, 1, 1, 2) times—20 (22, 24, 26, 24) sts rem.

NEXT ROW (WS): BO 2 sts, work to end—2 sts dec'd.

Work 1 RS row.

Rep the last 2 rows 1 (1, 2, 2, 1) times—16 (18, 18, 20, 20) sts rem.

Cont working even as est until armhole measures 7¾ (8, 8½, 8¾, 9)" (19.5 [20.5, 21.5, 22, 23] cm) from divide, ending after a WS row.

Place all sts onto st holders or waste yarn. Break yarn, leaving a tail at least 1 yd (91.5 cm) long.

Sleeve

With smaller needle, CO 48 (52, 56, 58, 62) sts. Divide the sts evenly over 3 or 4 dpn. Pm for beg of rnd and join for working in the rnd, being careful not to twist sts.

Work in twisted 1×1 rib until piece measures 2½" (6.5 cm) from beg.

Change to larger needles. Work in St st (knit all sts, every rnd) until piece measures 4" (10 cm) from beg.

Shape Sleeve

INC RND: K1, M1L (see Techniques), knit to last st, M1R (see Techniques), k1—2 sts inc'd.

Knit 7 (5, 4, 3, 3) rnds even.

Rep the last 8 (6, 6, 4, 4) rnds 7 (10, 12, 16, 17) times, then work inc rnd once more—66 (76, 84, 94, 100) sts.

Work even in St st until piece measures 15" (38 cm) from beg, ending 5 (6, 7, 8, 9) sts before the beg of rnd m.

Shape Cap

NEXT RND: BO next 10 (12, 14, 16, 18) sts removing m, knit to end—56 (64, 70, 78, 82) sts rem. Cont working back and forth in rows.

Purl 1 WS row.

DEC ROW (RS): K2, k2tog, knit to last 4 sts, ssk, k2—2 sts dec'd.

Rep the last 2 rows 5 (6, 7, 8, 9) times—44 (50, 54, 60, 62) sts rem.

[Work 3 rows even, then rep dec row] 4 (4, 3, 2, 1) times—36 (42, 48, 56, 60) sts rem.

[Purl 1 WS row, then rep dec row] 9 (9, 10, 11, 12) times—18 (24, 28, 34, 36) sts rem.

DEC ROW (WS): P2, ssp, purl to last 4 sts, p2tog, p2—2 sts dec'd.

Rep dec row on RS.

Rep the last 2 rows once more—10 (16, 20, 26, 28) sts rem.

BO rem sts.

Make a second sleeve the same as the first.

Finishing

Block pieces to measurements.

Join Shoulders

Return 16 (18, 18, 20, 20) held sts from left front and back shoulders onto larger needle and with RS facing each other, WS facing out, join the back and front shoulders together using the three-needle BO (see Techniques). Rep for right front and back shoulder. Set in sleeves, easing the cap into place.

Neckband

With 16" (40 cm) cir, beg at shoulder, pick up and knit 108 (108, 116, 116, 122) sts around neck edge. Pm for beg of rnd and join for working in the rnd. Work in twisted 1×1 rib for 5 rnds. BO all sts loosely in rib.

Weave in all ends. Block again if desired.

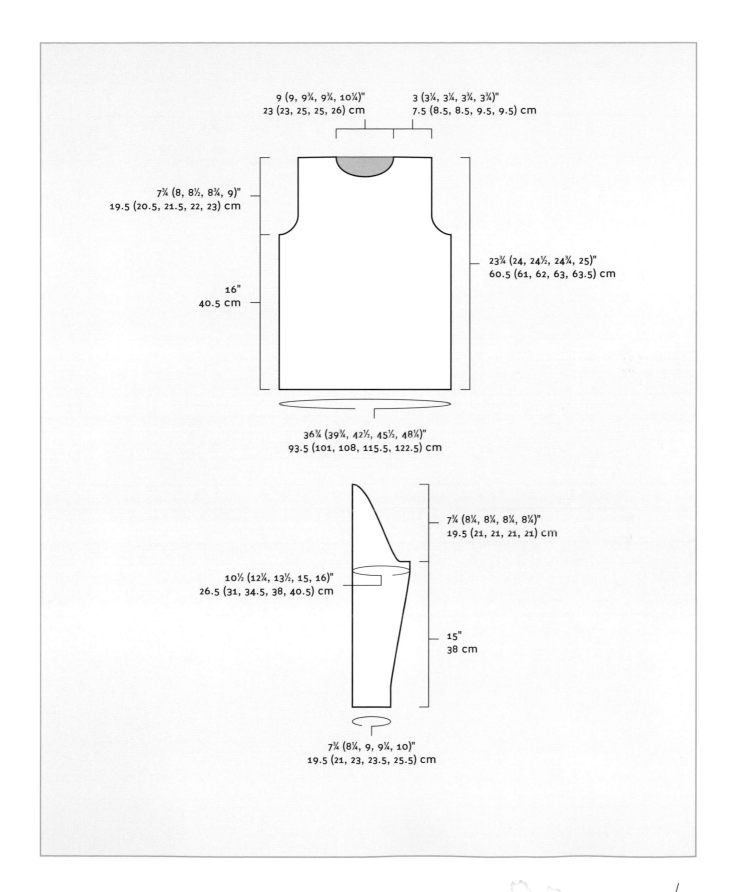

9 (9, 9¾, 9¾, 10¼)"
23 (23, 25, 25, 26) cm

3 (3¼, 3¼, 3¾, 3¾)"
7.5 (8.5, 8.5, 9.5, 9.5) cm

7¾ (8, 8½, 8¾, 9)"
19.5 (20.5, 21.5, 22, 23) cm

23¾ (24, 24½, 24¾, 25)"
60.5 (61, 62, 63, 63.5) cm

16"
40.5 cm

36¾ (39¾, 42½, 45½, 48¼)"
93.5 (101, 108, 115.5, 122.5) cm

7¾ (8¼, 8¼, 8¼, 8¼)"
19.5 (21, 21, 21, 21) cm

10½ (12¼, 13½, 15, 16)"
26.5 (31, 34.5, 38, 40.5) cm

15"
38 cm

7¾ (8¼, 9, 9¼, 10)"
19.5 (21, 23, 23.5, 25.5) cm

benton CARDIGAN

FINISHED SIZE

About 38 (42, 46, 50, 54)" (96.5 [106.5, 117, 127, 137] cm) bust circumference, with 3½" (9 cm) opening at front.

Cardigan shown measures 38" (96.5 cm).

YARN

Worsted weight (#4 medium).

SHOWN HERE: O-Wool Classic Worsted (100% wool; 99 yd [90 m]/50 g): #5401 Garnet, 12 (14, 15, 16, 17) skeins.

NEEDLES

BODY—Size U.S. 9 (5.5 mm): 32" (80 cm) circular (cir) and 4 or 5 double-pointed (dpn).

EDGING—Size U.S. 8 (5 mm): 32" (80 cm) cir and set of 4 or 5 dpn.

Adjust needle sizes if necessary to obtain the correct gauge.

NOTIONS

Stitch markers (m); stitch holders or waste yarn; cable needle (cn); tapestry needle.

GAUGE

16 sts and 21 rows = 4" (10 cm) in St st on larger needles.

26 sts = 4½" (11.5 cm) in Front charts on larger needles.

Bold modern cables, evocative of the depth and swirls of a Thomas Hart Benton painting, really pop in O-Wool Classic Worsted. This cardigan is worked seamlessly from the bottom up with a hybrid of raglan and set-in sleeve shaping that transitions to a cozy shawl collar. I chose to leave this cardigan open, but a few buttonholes can be added to the front band if you prefer a cardi with closure.

NOTE: *Circular needle is used to accommodate a large number of stitches. Do not join; work back and forth in rows.*

Sleeve

With smaller needle, CO 40 (44, 44, 48, 52) sts. Divide sts evenly over 3 or 4 smaller dpn, place marker (pm), and join for working in the rnd, being careful not to twist sts.

EST RIB: *K1, p2, k1, rep from *.

Rep the last rnd until piece measures 3¾" (9.5 cm) from CO.

Change to larger dpn and St st (knit every rnd).

Shape Sleeve

Knit 11 (11, 7, 7, 7) rnds.

INC RND: K1, M1L (see Techniques), knit to last st, M1R (see Techniques), k1–2 sts inc'd.

Rep the last 12 (12, 8, 8, 8) rnds 4 (5, 7, 8, 8) times–50 (56, 60, 66, 70) sts.

Work even until piece measures 19" (48.5 cm) from CO, ending 3 (3, 4, 6, 7) sts before the end of rnd. Break yarn, leaving at least a 9" (23 cm) tail, and place the next 6 (6, 8, 12, 14) sts onto st holder or waste yarn for underarm. Place the rem 44 (50, 52, 54, 56) onto st holder or waste yarn for the yoke.

Make a second sleeve the same as the first.

Body

With smaller cir, CO 156 (172, 188, 204, 220) sts. Do not join; work back and forth in rows.

EST RIB (WS): P2, *p1, k2, p1; rep from * to last 2 sts, p2.

NEXT ROW (RS): K2, *k1, p2, k1; rep from * to last 2 sts, k2.

Rep the last 2 rows until piece measures 2¼" (5.5 cm), ending after a WS row.

Change to larger cir.

EST FRONT CHARTS (RS): Work 3 sts in St st, 26 sts in Right Front chart, 11 (15, 19, 23, 27) sts in St st, pm for side, work 76 (84, 92, 100, 108) sts in St st, pm for side, work 11 (15, 19, 23, 27) sts in St st, 26 sts in Left Front chart, 3 sts in St st.

Shape Waist

Work 11 rows even as est, ending after a WS row.

DEC ROW (RS): *Work as est to 3 sts before m, ssk, k1, sl m, k1, k2tog; rep from * once more, work to end as est–4 sts dec'd.

Rep the last 12 rows 2 times–144 (160, 176, 192, 208) sts.

Work 11 rows even as est, ending after a WS row.

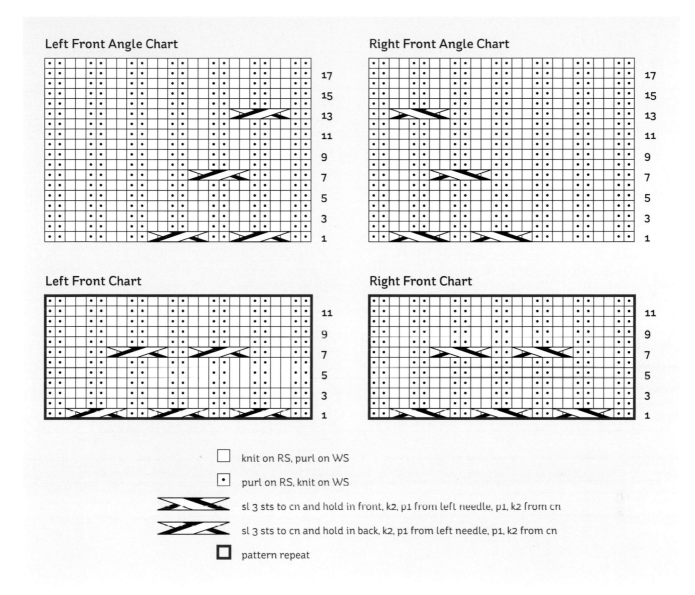

Left Front Angle Chart

Right Front Angle Chart

Left Front Chart

Right Front Chart

☐ knit on RS, purl on WS

• purl on RS, knit on WS

sl 3 sts to cn and hold in front, k2, p1 from left needle, p1, k2 from cn

sl 3 sts to cn and hold in back, k2, p1 from left needle, p1, k2 from cn

■ pattern repeat

INC ROW (RS): *Work as est to 1 st before m, M1R, k1, sl m, k1, M1R; rep from * once more, work to end as est—4 sts inc'd.

Work 5 rows even as est, ending after a WS row.

Rep the last 6 rows 2 times—156 (172, 188, 204, 220) sts.

Cont working as est until six 12-row repeats of the Front charts are completed, ending after WS Row 12. Piece measures about 16" (40.5 cm).

EST FRONT ANGLE CHARTS (RS): Work 3 sts in St st, 26 sts in Right Front Angle chart, work in St st to Left Front chart, work 26 sts in Left Front Angle chart, work 3 sts in St st.

Cont working even as est until piece measures 18" (45.5 cm) from CO, ending after a WS row.

Yoke

NOTE: *While working yoke, cont working Front Angle charts until all 18 rows are completed, then continue working those 26 sts in ribbing as est.*

JOINING ROW (RS): Work 37 (41, 44, 46, 49) right front sts, place the next 6 (6, 8, 12, 14) sts onto st holder or waste yarn for underarm, pm, return 44 (50, 52, 54, 56) held sleeve sts onto dpn and work across, pm and work 70 (78, 84, 88, 94) back sts, place the next 6 (6, 8, 12, 14) sts onto st holder or waste yarn for underarm, pm, return 44 (50, 52, 54, 56) held sleeve sts to dpn and work across, pm, and work rem 37 (41, 44, 46, 49) left front sts to end–232 (260, 276, 288, 304) sts.

Work 1 WS row even as est.

Shape Raglan

FRONT, BACK, AND SLEEVE DEC ROW (RS): *Work to 3 sts before next m, ssk, k1, sl m, k1, k2tog; rep from * 3 more times, work to end–8 sts dec'd.

Work 1 WS row even as est.

Rep the last 2 rows 5 (9, 12, 14, 17) times–184 (180, 172, 168, 160) sts rem: 31 sts each front, 32 (30, 26, 24, 20) sts each sleeve, and 58 sts for back.

BACK AND SLEEVE DEC ROW (RS): Work as est to m, *sl m, k1, k2tog, work to 3 sts before next m, ssk, k1, sl m; rep from * 2 more times, work to end as est–6 sts dec'd.

Work 3 rows even as est.

Rep the last 4 rows 1 (0, 0, 0, 0) times–172 (174, 166, 162, 154) sts rem: 31 sts each front, 28 (28, 24, 22, 18) sts each sleeve, and 54 (56, 56, 56, 56) sts for back.

[Work back and sleeve dec row, then work 1 WS row even] 12 (12, 10, 9, 7) times– 100 (102, 106, 108, 112) sts rem: 31 sts each front, 4 sts each sleeve, and 30 (32, 36, 38, 42) sts for back.

Shape Neck

NEXT ROW (RS): Work 31 sts as est for right neck, BO the next 38 (40, 44, 46, 50) sts, work rem 31 sts as est for

left neck. Continue working back and forth on the left neck sts, keeping the right neck sts on needle to be worked later.

Left Neck Extension

Work in rib as est until piece measures 4¼ (4½, 5, 5¼, 5¾)" (11 [11.5, 12.5, 13.5, 14.5] cm) from neck BO. Place left neck extension sts on a st holder or waste yarn and break yarn.

Right Neck Extension

Rejoin yarn to right neck sts, preparing to work a WS row. Work the same as the left neck extension.

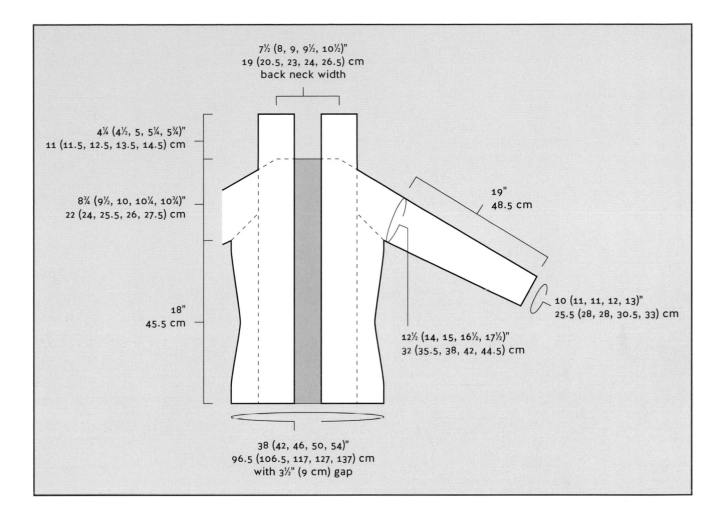

7½ (8, 9, 9½, 10½)"
19 (20.5, 23, 24, 26.5) cm
back neck width

4¼ (4½, 5, 5¼, 5¾)"
11 (11.5, 12.5, 13.5, 14.5) cm

8¾ (9½, 10, 10¼, 10¾)"
22 (24, 25.5, 26, 27.5) cm

19"
48.5 cm

18"
45.5 cm

10 (11, 11, 12, 13)"
25.5 (28, 28, 30.5, 33) cm

12½ (14, 15, 16½, 17½)"
32 (35.5, 38, 42, 44.5) cm

38 (42, 46, 50, 54)"
96.5 (106.5, 117, 127, 137) cm
with 3½" (9 cm) gap

Finishing

Block piece to measurements.

Return held neck extension sts onto two needles and join them together by grafting in rib (see Techniques).

With yarn threaded on a tapestry needle, sew selvedge edge of neck extensions to the BO neck edge, stretching the extensions gently to fit.

Return the held underarm sts to the needles and use the 9" (23 cm) tail from the sleeve and the Kitchener st (see Techniques) to graft sleeve and body sts together.

Front band

With smaller cir, beg at right front hem, pick up and knit 250 (254, 258, 262, 270) sts (about 3 sts for every 4 rows) along front edge up the right front, along the neck back, and down the left front.

EST RIB (WS): P2, *k2, p2; rep from *.

NEXT ROW (RS): K2, *p2, k2; rep from *.

Rep the last 2 rows once more, then work one more WS row.

BO all sts in rib.

Weave in ends.

Block again if desired.

remington CARDIGAN

FINISHED SIZE

About 35 (38¼, 41½, 44¾, 47¾)" (89 [97, 105.5, 113.5, 121.5] cm) bust circumference, buttoned, with ¾" (2 cm) overlapping buttonband.

Cardigan shown measures 35" (89 cm).

YARN

Worsted weight (#4 medium).

SHOWN HERE: Swans Island Natural Colors Worsted (100% wool; 250 yd [229 m]/100 g): Logwood, 5 (5, 5, 6, 6) skeins.

NEEDLES

BODY—Size U.S. 6 (4 mm): 24" (60 cm) circular (cir) and set of 4 or 5 double-pointed (dpn).

EDGING—Size U.S. 4 (3.5 mm): 24" (60 cm) cir and set of 4 or 5 dpn.

Adjust needle sizes if necessary to obtain the correct gauge.

NOTIONS

Stitch markers (m); stitch holders or waste yarn; tapestry needle; six ⅝" (1.5 cm) buttons.

GAUGE

20 sts and 27 rows = 4" (10 cm) in St st on larger needles.

The feather motif on this cardigan—named for Frederic Remington, the painter and sculptor who shaped the romantic image of the American Old West—is actually more than a decorative element. The V-neck is formed with fully fashioned dart shaping rather than the more traditional decreases at the neck edge. On the left front, the pattern is incorporated into a lace motif embellishment, and on the right, it's worked with a simple centered double decrease.

NOTE: *Circular needle is used to accommodate a large number of stitches. Do not join; work back and forth in rows.*

Body

With smaller cir, CO 179 (195, 211, 227, 243) sts, do not join.

Knit 5 rows.

Change to larger cir.

EST PATT (RS): Work 5 sts in garter st (knit all sts, every row) for buttonhole band, work 42 (46, 50, 54, 58) sts in St st (knit on RS, purl on WS) for right front, place marker (pm), work 85 (93, 101, 109, 117) sts in St st for the back, pm, work 42 (46, 50, 54, 58) sts in St st for left front, work last 5 sts in garter st for buttonband.

Work 5 rows even as est, ending after a WS row.

NOTE: *Read the following instructions before cont; waist is shaped before buttonholes are completed.*

BUTTONHOLE ROW (RS): (RS) K1, k2tog, yo, work to end as est.

Work 17 rows as est, ending after a WS row.

Rep the last 18 rows 4 times, then rep buttonhole row once more—6 buttonholes.

And at the same time, when piece measures 3½" (9 cm) from beg, end after a WS row.

Shape Waist

DEC ROW (RS): Work to 3 sts before m, ssk, k1, sl m, k2tog, work to 2 sts before the next m, ssk, sl m, k1, k2tog, work to end—4 sts dec'd.

Work 11 rows even, ending after a WS row.

Rep the last 12 rows once more—171 (187, 203, 219, 235) sts rem.

Cont working even as est until piece measures 9" (23 cm) from beg, ending after a WS row.

INC ROW (RS): Work to 1 st before m, M1R (see Techniques), k1, sl m, M1L (see Techniques), work to the next m, M1R, sl m, k1, M1L, work to end—4 sts inc'd.

Work 11 rows even, ending after a WS row.

Rep the last 12 rows once more—179 (195, 211, 227, 243) sts.

Cont working even until piece measures 14½" (37 cm) from beg, ending after a WS row.

EST PATT (RS): Work 5 buttonhole band sts as est, k15, place a movable m into the next st for neck shaping, [work to next m, sl m] twice, work 13 (17, 21, 25, 29) sts, pm for Lace chart, work 29 sts from Lace chart, pm, work 5 buttonband sts as est.

Work as est for 7 rows, ending after WS Row 8 of patt.

Right Slanting Chart

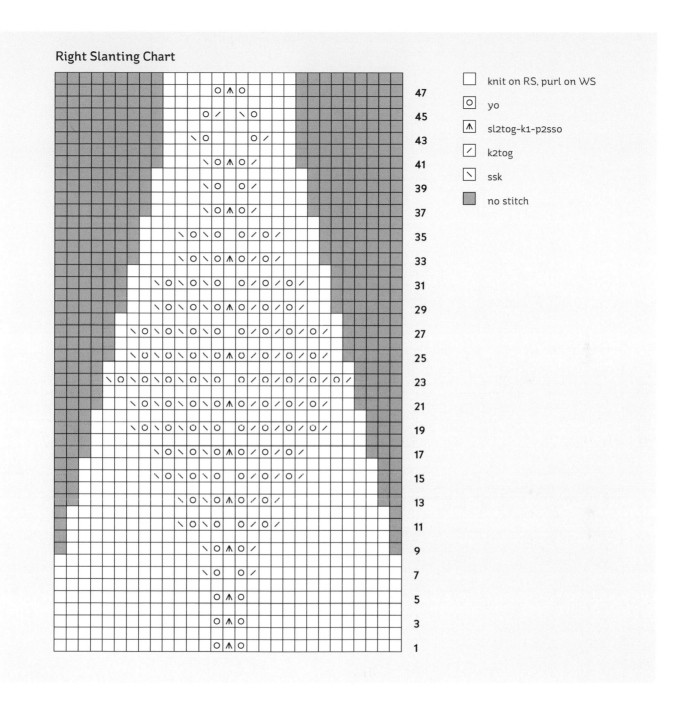

Legend:
- ☐ knit on RS, purl on WS
- ⊙ yo
- ⋀ sl2tog-k1-p2sso
- ╱ k2tog
- ╲ ssk
- ▨ no stitch

Shape Neck

NECK DEC ROW (RS): Work to 1 st before neck m, sl2tog-k1-p2sso (see Abbreviations), replace m into this st, work to end as est—175 (191, 207, 223, 239) total sts rem: 45 (49, 53, 57, 61) sts each front and 85 (93, 101, 109, 117) sts for back.

Work 1 WS row even as est.

Divide Back and Front

NEXT ROW (RS): Work to 5 (6, 7, 8, 9) sts before side m, BO next 9 (11, 13, 15, 17) sts removing m, work to 4 (5, 6, 7, 8) sts before side m, BO next 9 (11, 13, 15, 17) sts, removing m, work to end—40 (43, 46, 49, 52) sts rem each front, 77 (83, 89, 95, 101) sts rem for back.

Cont working back and forth on left front sts only. Place sts for right front and back onto st holder or waste yarn.

Left Front

Cont working Lace chart as est while working as foll:

NOTE: *St count changes from chart are incorporated into the st counts listed.*

Shape Armhole

Purl 1 WS row.

DEC ROW (RS): K1, k2tog, work to end as est—1 st dec'd at armhole.

Rep last 2 rows 4 (5, 5, 5, 6) times, ending after RS Row 21 (23, 23, 23, 25) of patt—29 (31, 34, 37, 37) sts rem.

Cont working as est until Row 48 of Lace chart is completed—19 (21, 24, 27, 29) sts rem.

EST PATT (RS): Work in St st to last 5 sts, work 5 buttonband sts as est.

Cont working even as est until armhole measures 7 (7½, 8, 8½, 9)" (18 [19, 20.5, 21.5, 23] cm) from divide, ending after a WS row.

Shape Shoulder

NEXT ROW (RS): BO 4 (5, 6, 7, 8) sts, work to end—15 (16, 18, 20, 21) sts rem.

Work 1 WS row even.

Rep the last 2 rows once more—11 (11, 12, 13, 13) sts rem.

NEXT ROW (RS): BO 6 (6, 7, 8, 8) sts, work to end—5 sts rem.

Front Band Extension

Work rem 5 sts in garter st for 19 (23, 23, 23, 25) rows, ending after a WS row.

Place sts onto a st holder or waste yarn. Break yarn.

Back

Return 77 (83, 89, 95, 101) held back sts to larger needle and join yarn, preparing to work a WS row.

Shape Armholes

Purl 1 WS row even.

DEC ROW (RS): K1, k2tog, knit to last 3 sts, ssk, k1—2 sts dec'd.

Rep the last 2 rows 4 (5, 5, 5, 6) times—67 (71, 77, 83, 87) sts rem.

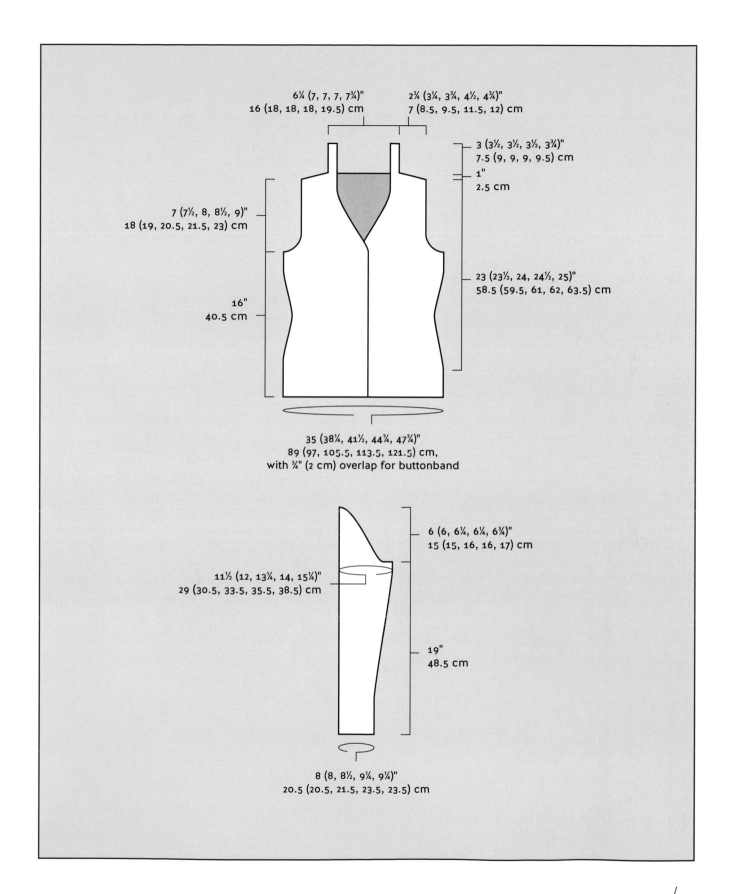

6¼ (7, 7, 7, 7¾)"
16 (18, 18, 18, 19.5) cm

2¾ (3¼, 3¾, 4½, 4¾)"
7 (8.5, 9.5, 11.5, 12) cm

3 (3½, 3½, 3½, 3¾)"
7.5 (9, 9, 9, 9.5) cm

1"
2.5 cm

7 (7½, 8, 8½, 9)"
18 (19, 20.5, 21.5, 23) cm

23 (23½, 24, 24½, 25)"
58.5 (59.5, 61, 62, 63.5) cm

16"
40.5 cm

35 (38¼, 41½, 44¾, 47¾)"
89 (97, 105.5, 113.5, 121.5) cm,
with ¾" (2 cm) overlap for buttonband

6 (6, 6¼, 6¼, 6¾)"
15 (15, 16, 16, 17) cm

11½ (12, 13¼, 14, 15¼)"
29 (30.5, 33.5, 35.5, 38.5) cm

19"
48.5 cm

8 (8, 8½, 9¼, 9¼)"
20.5 (20.5, 21.5, 23.5, 23.5) cm

Cont working even in St st until armholes measure 7 (7½, 8, 8½, 9)" (18 [19, 20.5, 21.5, 23] cm) from divide, ending after a WS row.

Shape Shoulders

BO 4 (5, 6, 7, 8) sts at the beg of the next 4 rows, then 6 (6, 7, 8, 8) sts at beg of next 2 rows—31 (35, 35, 35, 39) sts rem. BO all rem sts. Break yarn.

Right Front

Return 40 (43, 46, 49, 52) held right front sts to larger needle and join yarn, preparing to work a WS row.

Shape Neck and Armholes

Work 1 WS row.

ARMHOLE AND NECK DEC ROW (RS): Work to 1 st before marked neck st, sl2tog-k1-p2sso, replace m into this st, work to last 3 sts, ssk, k1—3 sts dec'd.

Work 1 WS row.

ARMHOLE DEC ROW (RS): Work to last 3 sts, ssk, k1—1 st dec'd.

Rep the last 4 rows 1 (2, 2, 2, 2) times—30 (31, 34, 37, 38) sts rem.

Sizes 35 (47¾)" only

Work 1 WS row, then rep armhole and neck dec row—29 (37) sts rem.

All Sizes

Work 1 (3, 3, 3, 1) rows even, ending after a WS row.

Shape Neck

NECK DEC ROW (RS): Work to 1 st before marked neck st, sl2tog-k1-p2sso, replace m into this st, work to end as est—2 sts dec'd.

Work 3 rows even as est, ending ater a WS row.

Rep the last 4 rows 4 (4, 4, 4, 3) times—19 (21, 24, 27, 29) sts rem.

Cont working even as est until armhole measures 7 (7½, 8, 8½, 9)" (18 [19, 20.5, 21.5, 23] cm) from divide, ending after a RS row.

Shape Shoulder

NEXT ROW (WS): BO 4 (5, 6, 7, 8) sts, work to end—15 (16, 18, 20, 21) sts rem.

Work 1 RS row even.

Rep the last 2 rows once more—11 (11, 12, 13, 13) sts rem.

NEXT ROW (WS): BO 6 (6, 7, 8, 8) sts, work to end—5 sts rem.

Front Band Extension

Work rem 5 sts in garter st for 20 (24, 24, 24, 26) rows, ending after a WS row.

Place sts onto a st holder or waste yarn. Break yarn.

Sleeve

With smaller needles, CO 40 (40, 42, 46, 46). Divide sts evenly over 3 or 4 dpn. Pm for beg of rnd and join for working in the rnd, being careful not to twist sts.

RND 1: Purl 1 rnd.

RND 2: Knit 1 rnd.

Rep the last 2 rnds 2 times.

Change to larger dpn.

Work in St st (knit all sts, every rnd) until piece measures 2" (5 cm) from beg.

Shape Sleeve

INC RND: K1, M1L knit to end, M1R—2 sts inc'd.

Knit 11 (9, 7, 7, 5) rnds.

Rep the last 12 (10, 8, 8, 6) rnds 8 (9, 11, 11, 14) times—58 (60, 66, 70, 76) sts.

Work even until piece measures 19" (48.5 cm) from beg, ending last rnd 4 (5, 6, 7, 8) sts before the beg of rnd m.

Shape Cap

NEXT RND: BO 9 (11, 13, 15, 17) sts, knit to end—49 (49, 53, 55, 59) sts rem.
Cont working back and forth in rows as foll:

Purl 1 WS row.

DEC ROW (RS): K1, k2tog, knit to last 3 sts, ssk, k1—2 sts dec'd.

Rep the last 2 rows 4 (4, 5, 5, 6) times—39 (39, 41, 43, 45) sts rem.

[Work 3 rows even, then rep dec row] 4 (4, 3, 2, 1) time(s)—31 (31, 35, 39, 43) sts rem.

[Purl 1 WS row, then rep dec row] 4 (4, 6, 8, 10) times—23 sts rem.

DEC ROW (WS): P1, ssp, purl to last 3 sts, p2tog, p1—2 sts dec'd.

Rep dec row on RS—2 sts dec'd.

Rep the last 2 rows 2 times—11 sts.

BO rem sts.

Work second sleeve the same as the first.

Finishing

Block pieces to measurements.

With yarn threaded in a tapestry needle, sew shoulder sts. Set in sleeves, easing the caps into place.

Return held 5 band sts from each front to dpn and join with Kitchener st (see Techniques). Sew the selvedge edge of front bands to the back neck, easing to fit.

Weave in all ends.

Sew buttons opposite buttonholes. Block again if desired.

hopper CARDIGAN

FINISHED SIZE
About 36 (39½, 42¾, 46¼, 49½)" (91.5 [100.5, 108.5, 117.5, 125.5] cm) bust circumference, buttoned, with 1½" (3.8 cm) overlapped buttonband.

Cardigan shown measures 36" (91.5 cm).

YARN
Worsted weight (#4 medium).

SHOWN HERE: Quince and Co. Lark (100% wool; 134 yd [123 m]/50 g): Cypress, 9 (10, 11, 12, 13) skeins.

NEEDLES
BODY–Size U.S. 7 (4.5 mm): 24" (60 cm) circular (cir) and set of 4 or 5 double-pointed (dpn).

EDGING–Size U.S. 5 (3.75 mm): 24" (60 cm) cir and set of 4 or 5 dpn.

Adjust needle sizes if necessary to obtain the correct gauge.

NOTIONS
Movable stitch markers (m); cable needle (cn); stitch holders or waste yarn; tapestry needle; eight ¾" (2 cm) buttons.

GAUGE
19 sts and 25 rows = 4" (10 cm) in St st on larger needles.

Worked from the bottom up with sewn set-in sleeves, this cardigan features feminine princess seam lines created with a cable and eyelet motif. This classic silhouette gives the sweater a timeless quality that is conservative but not prim, like a a figure from an Edward Hopper painting.

NOTES

- *Circular needles are used to accommodate a large number of stitches. Do not join; work back and forth in rows.*

- *When decreasing chart stitches, be sure to work corresponding yarnovers and decreases in order to maintain the correct stitch count. If one is not worked, work the other in stockinette. If there are not enough stitches to work the full cable, work stitches in stockinette instead.*

Body

With smaller cir, CO 164 (180, 196, 212, 228) sts. Do not join; work back and forth in rows.

EST RIB (WS): P1, *p2, k2; rep from * to last 3 sts, p3.

NEXT ROW (RS): K1, *k2, p2; rep from * to last 3 sts, k3.

Rep the last 2 rows until piece measures 2½" (6.5 cm) from beg, ending after a WS row.

Change to larger cir.

EST PATT (RS): Work 15 (15, 19, 19, 23) sts in St st (knit on RS, purl on WS), pm, work 8 sts from Left Slanting chart, pm, work 34 (42, 42, 50, 50) sts in St st, pm, work 8 sts from Right Slanting chart, pm, work 34 (34, 42, 42, 50) sts in St st, pm, work 8 sts from Left Slanting chart, pm, work 34 (42, 42, 50, 50) sts in St st, pm, work 8 sts from Right Slanting chart, pm, work 15 (15, 19, 19, 23) sts in St st.

Work even as est until piece measures 4" (10 cm) from beg, ending after a WS row.

Shape Waist

DEC ROW (RS): *Knit to m, sl m, work 8 sts as est, sl m, ssk, knit to 2 sts before next m, k2tog, sl m, work 8 sts as est, sl m; rep from* once more, knit to end—4 sts dec'd.

Work 7 rows even, ending after a WS row.

Rep the last 8 rows once more—156 (172, 188, 204, 220) sts rem.

Work 8 rows even as est, ending after a WS row.

INC ROW (RS): *Knit to m, sl m, work 8 sts as est, sl m, k1, M1L (see Techniques), knit to 1 st before next m, M1R (see Techniques), k1, sl m, work 8 sts as est, sl m; rep from * once more, knit to end—4 sts inc'd.

Work 11 rows even as est, ending after a WS row.

Rep the last 12 rows once more—164 (180, 196, 212, 228) sts.

Work even as est until piece measures 16" (40.5 cm) from beg, ending after a WS row.

Divide Fronts and Back

NEXT ROW (RS): Work 35 (38, 41, 44, 47) sts as est for right front, BO next 10 (12, 14, 16, 18) sts, work 74 (80, 86, 92, 98) sts as est for back, BO next 10 (12, 14, 16, 18) sts, work 35 (38, 41, 44, 47) rem sts for left front.

Cont working back and forth on left front sts only. Place sts for the right front and back on st holder or waste yarn.

Left Front
Shape Armhole

Work 1 WS row even.

DEC ROW (RS): K1, k2tog, work to end as est—1 st dec'd.

Rep the last 2 rows 2 (3, 4, 5, 6) times—32 (34, 36, 38, 40) sts rem: 9 (11, 9, 11, 9) St sts on armhole edge of chart, 8 chart sts, 15 (15, 19, 19, 23) St sts on front edge of chart.

- -

NOTE: *Read the following instructions carefully before cont. Neck shaping beg before shifting the chart is completed.*

- -

Shift Chart

Work 1 WS row.

SHIFT ROW 1 (RS): Knit to 2 sts before m, k2tog, sl m, work 8 sts as est, sl m, k1, M1R, knit to end.

Rep the last 2 rows 7 (9, 7, 9, 7) times.

Work 1 WS row.

SHIFT ROW 2 (RS): K1, remove m, ssk, work as est to m (see Notes), sl m, k1, M1R, knit to end.

Rep the last 2 rows 7 times, removing the last m on the last rep, then work all sts in St st.

And at the same time, when armhole measures 3¼ (3½, 3¾, 4, 4¼)" (8.5 [9, 9.5, 10, 11] cm) from divide, end after a RS row.

Shape Neck

NEXT ROW (WS): BO 8 sts, work to end as est—24 (26, 28, 30, 32) sts rem.

Work 1 RS row as est.

NEXT ROW: BO 4 sts, work to end as est—20 (22, 24, 26, 28) sts rem.

Work 1 RS row as est.

NEXT ROW: BO 3 sts, work to end as est—17 (19, 21, 23, 25) sts rem.

Work 1 RS row as est.

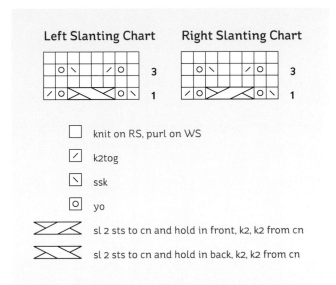

Left Slanting Chart   **Right Slanting Chart**

□ knit on RS, purl on WS

⟋ k2tog

⟍ ssk

○ yo

⤢ sl 2 sts to cn and hold in front, k2, k2 from cn

⤢ sl 2 sts to cn and hold in back, k2, k2 from cn

NEXT ROW: BO 2 sts, work to end as est—15 (17, 19, 21, 23) sts rem.

Work 1 RS row as est.

NEXT ROW (WS): BO 1 st, work to end as est—14 (16, 18, 20, 22) sts rem.

Work 1 RS row as est.

Rep the last 2 rows 1 (1, 2, 3, 3) times—12 (14, 15, 16, 18) sts rem.

Cont working as est until armhole measures 7¾ (8, 8¼, 8½, 8¾)" (19.5 [20.5, 21, 21.5, 22] cm) from divide, ending after a RS row.

Shape Shoulder with Short-Rows

SHORT-ROW 1 (WS): Purl to last 4 (5, 5, 5, 6) sts, wrap next st, and turn so RS is facing.

Knit 1 RS row.

SHORT-ROW 2 (WS): Purl to last 8 (10, 10, 10, 12) sts, wrap next st, and turn so RS is facing.

Knit 1 RS row.

NEXT ROW (WS): Purl to end, picking up the wraps and working them together with the sts they wrap as they appear. Break yarn and place sts onto st holder or waste yarn.

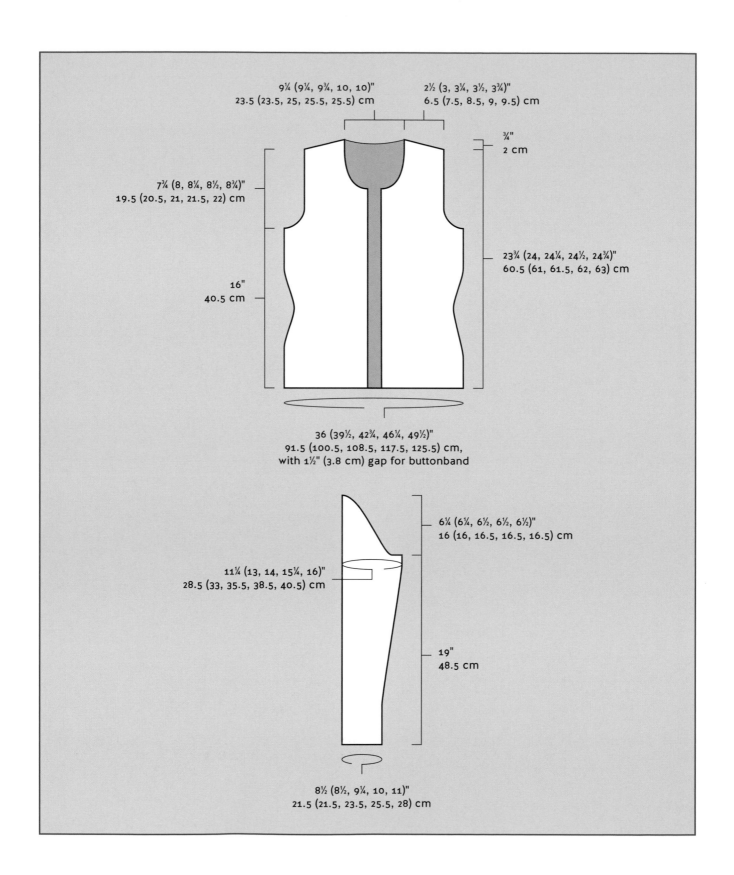

9¼ (9¼, 9¾, 10, 10)"
23.5 (23.5, 25, 25.5, 25.5) cm

2½ (3, 3¼, 3½, 3¾)"
6.5 (7.5, 8.5, 9, 9.5) cm

¾"
2 cm

7¾ (8, 8¼, 8½, 8¾)"
19.5 (20.5, 21, 21.5, 22) cm

23¾ (24, 24¼, 24½, 24¾)"
60.5 (61, 61.5, 62, 63) cm

16"
40.5 cm

36 (39½, 42¾, 46¼, 49½)"
91.5 (100.5, 108.5, 117.5, 125.5) cm,
with 1½" (3.8 cm) gap for buttonband

6¼ (6¼, 6½, 6½, 6½)"
16 (16, 16.5, 16.5, 16.5) cm

11¼ (13, 14, 15¼, 16)"
28.5 (33, 35.5, 38.5, 40.5) cm

19"
48.5 cm

8½ (8½, 9¼, 10, 11)"
21.5 (21.5, 23.5, 25.5, 28) cm

Back

Return 74 (80, 86, 92, 98) held back sts onto larger needle and join yarn, preparing to work a WS row.

Shape Armholes

Work 1 WS row even.

DEC ROW (RS): K1, k2tog, work to last 3 sts as est, ssk, k1—2 sts dec'd.

Rep the last 2 rows 2 (3, 4, 5, 6) times—68 (72, 76, 80, 84) sts rem: 9 (11, 9, 11, 9) St sts at armhole edges of charts, 8 sts each chart, 34 (34, 42, 42, 50) St sts in center of charts.

Shift Charts

Work 1 WS row.

SHIFT ROW 1 (RS): Knit to 2 sts before m, k2tog, sl m, work 8 sts as est, sl m, k1, M1R, knit to 1 sts before next m, M1L, k1, work 8 sts at est, sl m, ssk, knit to end.

Rep the last 2 rows 7 (9, 7, 9, 7) times—1 St st rem at armhole edges of charts, 8 sts each chart, 50 (54, 58, 62, 66) sts in center of charts.

Work 1 WS row.

SHIFT ROW 2 (RS): K1, remove m, ssk, work as est to m (see Notes), sl m, k1, M1R, knit to 1 st before next m, M1L, k1, sl m, work to last 3 sts as est, k2tog, remove m, k1.

Rep the last 2 rows 7 times, removing the last markers on the last rep.

Work even in St st until armholes measure 7¼ (7½, 7¾, 8, 8¼)" (18.5 [19, 19.5, 20.5, 21] cm) from divide, ending after a WS row.

Shape Shoulders with Short-Rows

SHORT-ROW 1 (RS): Knit to last 4 (5, 5, 5, 6) sts, wrap next st, and turn so WS is facing; (WS) purl to last 4 (5, 5, 5, 6) sts, wrap next st, and turn so RS is facing.

SHORT-ROW 2 (RS): Knit to last 8 (10, 10, 10, 12) sts, wrap next st, and turn so WS is facing; (WS) purl to last 8 (10, 10, 10, 12) sts, wrap next st, and turn so RS is facing.

NEXT ROW (RS): Knit to end, picking up the wraps and working them together with the sts they wrap as they appear.

Shape Neck

NEXT ROW (WS): P12 (14, 15, 16, 18), BO next 44 (44, 46, 48, 48) sts, p12 (14, 15, 16, 18) sts, picking up the wraps and working them together with the sts they wrap as they appear. Break yarn and place sts onto st holder or waste yarn.

Right Front

Return 35 (38, 41, 44, 47) held right front sts onto larger needle and join yarn, preparing to work a WS row.

Shape Armhole

Work 1 WS row even.

DEC ROW (RS): Work to last 3 sts as est, ssk, k1—1 st dec'd.

Rep the last 2 rows 2 (3, 4, 5, 6) times—32 (34, 36, 38, 40) sts rem: 15 (15, 19, 19, 23) St sts on front edge of chart, 8 chart sts, 9 (11, 9, 11, 9) St sts on armhole edge of chart.

NOTE: *Read the following instructions carefully before cont. Neck shaping beg before shifting the chart is completed.*

Shift Chart

Work 1 WS row.

SHIFT ROW 1 (RS): Knit to 1 st before m, M1L, k1, sl m, work 8 sts as est, sl m, ssk, knit to end.

Rep the last 2 rows 7 (9, 7, 9, 7) times.

Work 1 WS row.

SHIFT ROW 2 (RS): Knit to 1 st before m, M1L, k1, sl m, work as est to last 3 sts (see Notes), k2tog, remove m, k1.

Rep the last 2 rows 7 times removing the last m on the last rep, then work all sts in St st.

And at the same time, when armhole measures 3¼ (3½, 3¾, 4, 4¼)" (8.5 [9, 9.5, 10, 11] cm) from divide, end after a WS row.

Shape Neck

NEXT ROW (RS): BO 8 sts, work to end as est—24 (26, 28, 30, 32) sts rem.

Work 1 WS row as est.

NEXT ROW: BO 4 sts, work to end as est—20 (22, 24, 26, 28) sts rem.

Work 1 WS row as est.

NEXT ROW: BO 3 sts, work to end as est—17 (19, 21, 23, 25) sts rem.

Work 1 WS row as est.

NEXT ROW: BO 2 sts, work to end as est—15 (17, 19, 21, 23) sts rem.

Work 1 WS row as est.

NEXT ROW (RS): BO 1 st, work to end as est—14 (16, 18, 20, 22) sts rem.

Work 1 WS row as est.

Rep the last 2 rows 1 (1, 2, 3, 3) times—12 (14, 15, 16, 18) sts rem.

Cont working as est until armhole measures 7¾ (8, 8¼, 8½, 8¾)" (19.5 [20.5, 21, 21.5, 22] cm) from divide, ending after a WS row.

Shape Shoulder with Short-Rows

SHORT-ROW 1 (RS): Knit to last 4 (5, 5, 5, 6) sts, wrap next st, and turn so WS is facing.

Purl 1 WS row.

SHORT-ROW 2 (RS): Knit to last 8 (10, 10, 10, 12) sts, wrap next st, and turn so WS is facing.

Purl 1 WS row.

NEXT ROW (RS): Knit to end, picking up the wraps and working them together with the sts they wrap as they appear. Break yarn and place sts onto st holder or waste yarn.

Sleeve

With smaller needle, CO 40 (40, 44, 48, 52) sts. Divide sts evenly over 3 or 4 smaller dpn. Pm and join for working in the rnd, being careful not to twist sts.

EST RIB: *K1, p2, k1; rep from *.

Rep the last rnd until piece measures 2½" (6.5 cm) from beg.

Change to larger dpn and work in St st (knit all sts, every rnd) until piece measures 4½" (11.5 cm) from beg.

Shape Sleeve

INC RND: K1, M1L, knit to last st, M1R, k1—2 sts inc'd.

Work 11 (7, 7, 5, 5) rnds even.

Rep the last 12 (8, 8, 6, 6) rnds 6 (10, 10, 11, 11) times—54 (62, 66, 72, 76) sts.

Work even until sleeve measures 19" (48.5 cm) from beg, ending 5 (6, 7, 8, 9) sts before end of last rnd.

Shape Cap

BO the next 10 (12, 14, 16, 18) sts, then knit to end—44 (50, 52, 56, 58) sts rem. Cont working back and forth in rows.

Purl 1 WS row.

DEC ROW (RS): K1, k2tog, knit to last 3 sts, ssk, k1—2 sts dec'd.

Rep the last 2 rows 3 (4, 4, 5, 5) times—36 (40, 42, 44, 46) sts rem.

[Work 3 rows even in St st, then rep dec row] 3 (2, 2, 1, 1) times—30 (36, 38, 42, 44) sts rem.

[Purl 1 WS row, then rep dec row] 7 (7, 8, 9, 9) times—16 (22, 22, 24, 26) sts rem.

DEC ROW (WS): P1, ssp, purl to last 3 sts, p2tog, p1—2 sts dec'd.

Work dec row on RS—2 sts dec'd.

Rep the last 2 rows 1 (2, 2, 2, 2) times—8 (10, 10, 12, 14) sts rem.

BO rem sts.

Make a second sleeve the same as the first.

Finishing

Block pieces to measurements. Return 12 (14, 15, 16, 18) held sts from left front and back shoulders onto larger needle and with RS facing each other, WS facing out, join the back and front shoulders together using the three-needle BO (see Techniques). Rep for right front and back shoulder. Set in sleeves, easing the cap into place.

Buttonband

With smaller cir, beg at neck edge of left front, pick up and knit 91 (91, 95, 95, 95) sts along front edge.

EST RIB (WS): *P2, k2; rep from * to last 3 sts, p3.

NEXT ROW (RS): K3, *p2, k2; rep from *.

Rep the last 2 rows 4 times. BO all sts in rib.

Buttonhole Band

Try on cardigan or lay flat to determine button placement: the top button will be placed in the neckband; the bottom button about 1–1¼" (2.5–3 cm) from the lower edge; and 6 more buttons placed evenly spaced between. Mark buttonhole placement on right front with movable st markers or waste yarn.

With smaller cir, beg at lower edge of right front, pick up and knit 91 (91, 95, 95, 95) sts along front edge.

EST RIB (WS): P3, *k2, p2; rep from *

NEXT ROW (RS): *K2, p2; rep from * to last 3 sts, k3.

Rep the last 2 rows once more.

BUTTONHOLE ROW (WS): *Work in rib as est to first m, yo, k2tog or p2tog keeping in patt; rep from * 6 more times, work to end in rib as est—7 buttonholes completed.

Work 5 rows even in rib as est. BO all sts in rib.

Neckband

With smaller cir, beg at right front buttonhole band edge, pick up and knit 122 (122, 126, 126, 130) sts evenly around neck and band edges.

EST RIB (WS): P2, *k2, p2; rep from *.

NEXT ROW (RS): K2, *p2, k2; rep from *.

Work 1 more row in rib as est.

BUTTONHOLE ROW (RS): Work 6 sts in rib as est, yo, p2tog, work rib to end.

Work 5 rows even in rib as est. BO all sts in rib.

Weave in ends, sew buttons to buttonband opposite buttonholes. Block again if desired.

tanner COWL

FINISHED SIZE
About 52¾" (134 cm) circumference and 10¾"
(27.5 cm) tall.

YARN
Worsted weight (#4 light).

SHOWN HERE: Manos Silk Blend (70% merino,
30% silk; 150 yd [137 m]/50 g): 300X Topaz: 3
skeins.

NEEDLES
Size U.S. 8 (5 mm): 24" (60 cm) circular (cir).

*Adjust needle size if necessary to obtain
the correct gauge.*

NOTIONS
Stitch marker (m); tapestry needle.

GAUGE
17 sts and 28 rnds = 4" (10 cm) in Lace chart.

This project is a good introduction to "knitted lace"—eyelets worked every row—because the cowl is worked in the round. I hesitate to say there is a right or wrong side to this piece because I love the way this stitch pattern looks on the purled side just as much as the knit side. The glowing ochre silk-blend yarn was chosen to give a Moroccan flavor to this cowl; the lace motif was likewise Moroccan-inspired by Henry Ossawa Tanner's painting *Gateway Tangier.* Tanner was an American artist who spent most of his career in the late nineteenth century working in Paris.

NOTE: *At beginning of Rounds 23, 27, 31, 35, 59, 63, and 67 of Lace chart, remove beginning-of-round marker, slip the last stitch of the round to the left needle, replace marker, then return the slipped stitch to right needle.*

Cowl

CO 224 sts. Place marker (pm) and join for working in the rnd, being careful not to twist sts.

Purl 3 rnds.

Work Rnds 1–69 of Lace chart.

Purl 3 rnds.

BO all sts pwise.

Finishing

Block to measurements.

Weave in ends.

Lace Chart

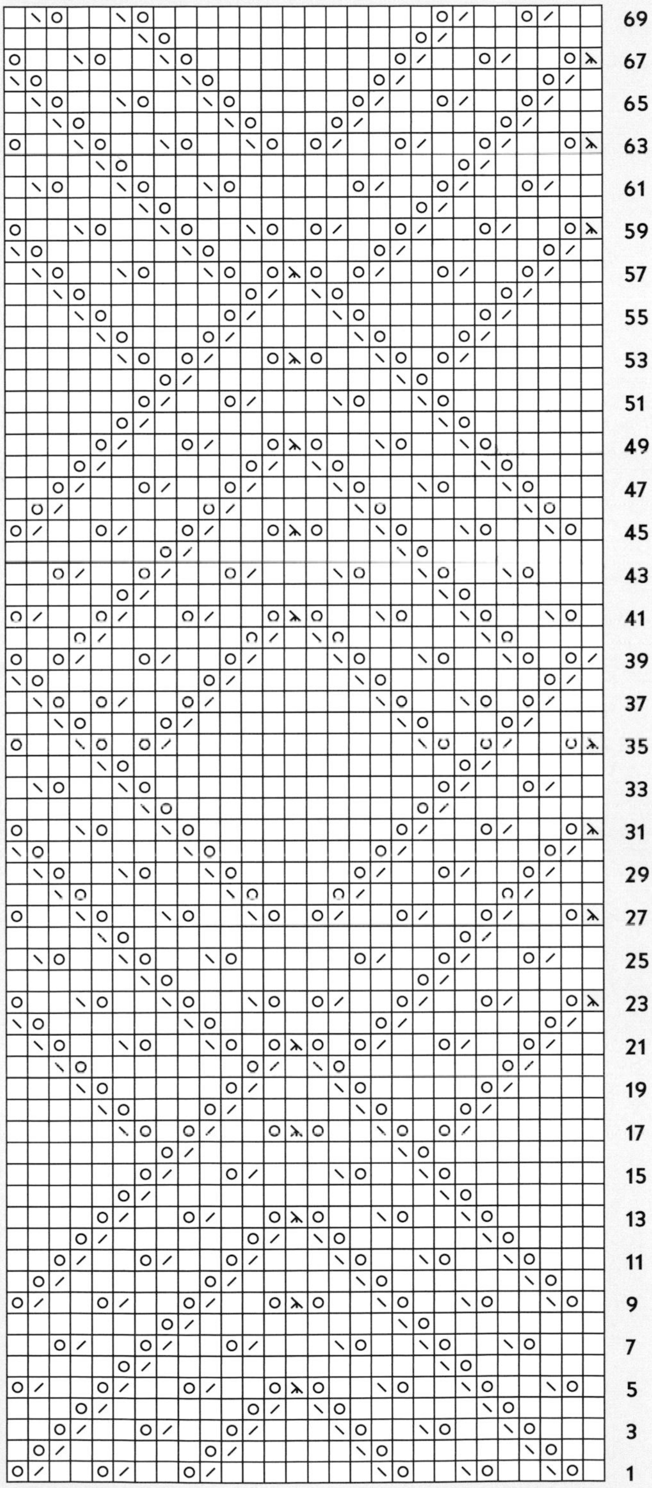
69
67
65
63
61
59
57
55
53
51
49
47
45
43
41
39
37
35
33
31
29
27
25
23
21
19
17
15
13
11
9
7
5
3
1

- knit
- yo
- ssk
- k2tog
- sl1-k2tog-psso
- At beg of rnd, remove beg-of-rnd m, sl last st of previous rnd to the left needle, replace beg-of-rnd m, return slipped st to right needle, k2tog, psso. On all other repeats: sl1-k2tog-psso.

parrish MITTS

FINISHED SIZE
About 7" (18 cm) in circumference and
7" (18 cm) long.

YARN
Worsted weight (#4 medium).

SHOWN HERE: Berroco Ultra Alpaca (50%
wool, 50% alpaca; 215 yd [197 m]/100 g):
#6280 Mahogany Mix (MC), #6288
Blueberry mix (CC), 1 skein each.

NEEDLES
Size U.S. 3 (3.25 mm): 1 set of 3 or 4 double-
pointed (dpn).

*Adjust needle sizes if necessary to obtain
the correct gauge.*

NOTIONS
Stitch marker (m); smooth waste yarn for
thumb placement; tapestry needle.

GAUGE
27 sts and 26 rnds = 4" (10 cm) in
Checkerboard chart worked in rnds.

The design of these mitts is a result of
color play in the palette of the painter and
illustrator Maxfield Parrish. Parrish began
every piece with a foundation of burnt umber
or ultramarine blue paint before building up
the image with translucent layers of color.
This gave his work a luminescent quality that
is unmistakable. The floral motif is inspired by
Pennsylvania Dutch folk art, also an influence
in Parrish's early illustration work.

Stitch Guide
Twisted Ribbing (multiple of 2 sts):
RND 1: *K1-tbl, p1-tbl; rep from *.

Rep Rnd 1 for patt.

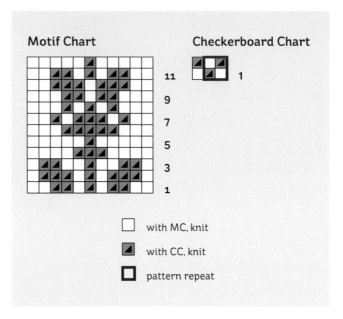

Motif Chart   Checkerboard Chart

☐ with MC, knit

◤ with CC, knit

☐ pattern repeat

Left Mitt

With MC, CO 48 sts. Divide sts evenly over 3 or 4 dpn. Place marker (pm) for beg of rnd and join for working in the rnd.

Work 4 rnds in twisted ribbing.

Knit 1 rnd.

EST PATT: Work 11 sts in Motif chart, work 37 sts in Checkerboard chart.

Cont working as est until Rnds 1–12 of Motif chart have been completed, then work Rnds 1–11 once more.

Place Thumb

NEXT RND: Work as est to last 7 sts, with waste yarn k7, sl 7 sts from right needle to the left needle, and cont working in Checkerboard chart to end.

Cont working as est until Rnd 11 of Motif chart is completed. Break CC.

With MC, knit 1 rnd.

Work 4 rnds twisted ribbing. BO all sts in ribbing.

Right Mitt

With MC, CO 48 sts. Divide sts evenly over 3 or 4 dpn. Pm for beg of rnd and join for working in the rnd.

Work 4 rnds in twisted ribbing.

Knit 1 rnd.

EST PATT: Work 37 sts in Checkerboard chart, work 11 sts in Motif chart.

Cont working as est until Rnds 1–12 of Motif chart have been completed, then work Rnds 1–11 once more.

Place Thumb

NEXT RND: With waste yarn k7, sl 7 sts from right needle to the left needle and cont working as est to end.

Cont working as est until Rnd 11 of Motif chart is completed. Break CC.

With MC, knit 1 rnd.

Work 4 rnds twisted ribbing. BO all sts in ribbing.

Thumb

Carefully remove the waste yarn from the thumb placement and place 7 sts onto each of 2 dpn. Distribute the sts as evenly as possible over 3 dpn and knit 1 rnd. Work 4 rnds twisted ribbing. BO all sts in ribbing.

Work thumb on second mitt the same as the first.

Finishing

Block to measurements.

Weave in ends.

edmonia T-SHIRT

FINISHED SIZE
About 34 (37¼, 40¾, 44, 47¼, 50¾)"
(86.5 [94.5, 103.5, 112, 120, 129] cm) bust
circumference.

Pullover shown measures 34" (86.5 m).

YARN
Sportweight (#2 fine).

SHOWN HERE: Manos Del Uruguay Serena
(60% baby alpaca, 40% pima cotton;
170 yd [155 m]/50 g): #2150 Fig, 4 (4, 5, 5,
6, 6) skeins.

NEEDLES
Size U.S. 4 (3.5 mm): 16" (40 cm) and 24"
(60 cm) circular (cir) and set of 4 or 5
double-pointed (dpn).

*Adjust needle sizes if necessary to obtain
the correct gauge.*

NOTIONS
Stitch markers (m); stitch holders or waste
yarn; tapestry needle.

GAUGE
24 sts and 27 rnds = 4" (10 cm) in St st,
worked in rnds.

The simple open neck and light drape of this
top-down pullover reminds me of the style of
blouse nineteenth-century sculptor Edmonia
Lewis might have worn. This alpaca-cotton-
blend top hits at the hip, with three-quarter
sleeves. It's a light sweater, but I'm already
imagining revisiting it to make a longer tunic
for multiseason layering piece or with short
sleeves for a beachy summer top.

NOTES

• The sweater is worked from the top down without seams.

• Markers are placed for raglan and on each side of the Lace charts. Use different-color markers to easily tell them apart.

NOTES

• Read the following instructions carefully before cont; Lace chart and raglan shaping are worked at the same time. Lace chart instructions change before raglan shaping is completed.

• Change to longer cir when sts no longer fit comfortably on shorter cir.

Yoke

With shorter cir, CO 116 sts. Place marker (pm) and join for working in the rnd, being careful not to twist sts.

Purl 1 rnd.

PLACE RAGLAN MARKERS: *K10 for sleeve, pm, k48 for front; rep from * once more.

Shape Raglan

EST PATT AND INC RND: *K1, LLI (see Techniques), work in St st (knit all sts, every rnd) to 1 st before m, RLI (see Techniques), k1, sl m, k1, LLI, k2, pm for Lace chart, work 42 sts in Lace chart, pm, k2, RLI, k1, sl m; rep from * once more—124 sts.

Rep Rnds 1–24 of Lace chart as est until 2 (2, 2, 2, 3, 3) reps are completed, then work Rnds 25–48 once. Once chart is completed, remove Lace chart markers and work all sts in St st; *and at the same time*, shape raglan as foll:

Work 1 rnd even as est.

INC RND: *K1, LLI, work as est to 1 st before next m, RLI, k1, sl m; rep from * 3 more times—8 sts inc'd.

Work 1 rnd even as est.

Rep the last 2 rnds 8 (14, 20, 31, 35, 39) times—196 (244, 292, 380, 412, 444) total sts: 30 (42, 54, 76, 84, 92) sts each sleeve, 68 (80, 92, 114, 122, 130) sts each front and back.

Lace Chart

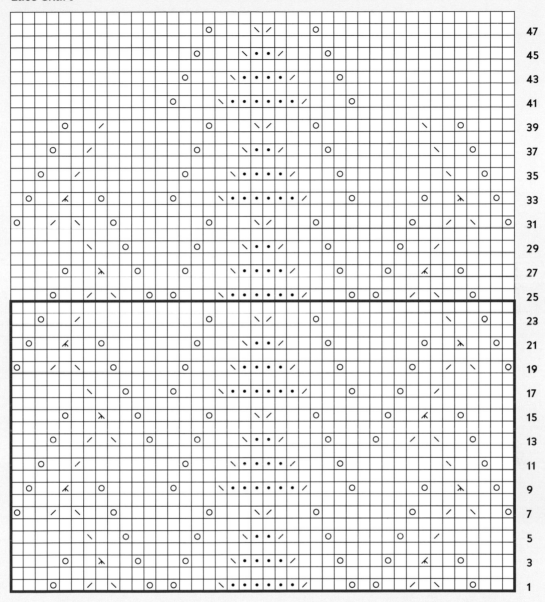

☐ knit	╱	k2tog
• purl	⼊	k3tog
⊙ yo	⼊	sssk
╲ ssk	◼	pattern repeat

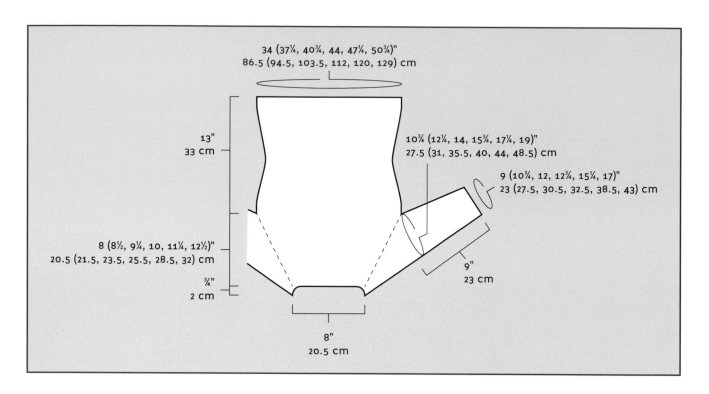

34 (37¼, 40¾, 44, 47¼, 50¾)"
86.5 (94.5, 103.5, 112, 120, 129) cm

13"
33 cm

10¾ (12¼, 14, 15¾, 17¼, 19)"
27.5 (31, 35.5, 40, 44, 48.5) cm

9 (10¾, 12, 12¾, 15¼, 17)"
23 (27.5, 30.5, 32.5, 38.5, 43) cm

8 (8½, 9¼, 10, 11¼, 12½)"
20.5 (21.5, 23.5, 25.5, 28.5, 32) cm

¾"
2 cm

9"
23 cm

8"
20.5 cm

Sizes 34 (37¼, 40¾)" only:

[Rep inc rnd, then work 3 rnds even] 5 (3, 1) times—236 (268, 300) total sts: 40 (48, 56) sts each sleeve, 78 (86, 94) sts each front and back.

[Rep inc rnd, then work 1 rnd even] 6 times—284 (316, 348) total sts: 52 (60, 68) sts each sleeve, 90 (98, 106) sts each front and back.

All Sizes
Divide Body and Sleeves

*Work 52 (60, 68, 76, 84, 92) sleeve sts, then place them onto a st holder or waste yarn, removing raglan markers, work 90 (98, 106, 114, 122, 130) sts for body; rep from * once more.

Body

JOINING RND: Use the backward-loop method (see Techniques) to CO 6 (7, 8, 9, 10, 11) sts, pm for beg of rnd, then CO another 6 (7, 8, 9, 10, 11) sts, work 90 (98, 106, 114, 122, 130) front sts as est, use the backward-loop method to CO 6 (7, 8, 9, 10, 11) sts, pm for side, then CO another 6 (7, 8, 9, 10, 11) sts, work 90 (98, 106, 114, 122, 130) back sts as est, then knit to beg of rnd m—204 (224, 244, 264, 284, 304) sts.

Cont working even as est until piece measures 3" (7.5 cm) from divide.

Shape Waist

DEC RND: *K1, k2tog, work as est to 3 sts before side m, ssk, k1, sl m; rep from * once more—4 sts dec'd.

Work 14 rnds even as est.

Rep dec rnd—196 (216, 236, 256, 276, 296) sts rem.

Work 8 rnds even as est.

INC RND: *K1, M1L, work as est to 1 st before side m, M1R, k1, sl m—4 sts inc'd.

Work 14 rnds even as est.

Rep the last 15 rnds once more—204 (224, 244, 264, 284, 304) sts.

Work even until piece measures 13" (33 cm) from divide. BO all sts pwise.

Sleeve

Distribute 52 (60, 68, 76, 84, 92) held sts from one sleeve evenly over dpn. With RS facing, beg at center of underarm sts, pick up and knit 6 (7, 8, 9, 10, 11) sts along half of the underarm CO sts, k52 (60, 68, 76, 84, 92) held sts, then pick up and knit 6 (7, 8, 9, 10, 11) sts from the CO underarm sts, pm for beg of rnd—64 (74, 84, 94, 104, 114) sts.

Work even in St st until piece measures 1" (2.5 cm).

Shape Sleeve

DEC RND: K1, k2tog, knit to last 3 sts, ssk, k1—2 sts dec'd.

Knit 9 (9, 7, 7, 7, 7) rnds.

Rep the last 10 (10, 8, 8, 8, 8) rnds 4 (4, 5, 5, 5, 5) times—54 (64, 72, 82, 92, 102) sts rem.

Work even until piece measures 9" (23 cm) from the underarm.

BO all sts pwise.

Work second sleeve the same as the first.

Finishing

Weave in all loose ends. Block to measurements.

evans TUNIC

INISHED SIZE

About 34½ (39, 44, 48½, 52)" (87.5 [99, 112, 123, 132] cm) bust circumference.

Pullover shown measures 34½" (87.5 cm).

YARN

Sportweight (#2 fine).

SHOWN HERE: Louet Euroflax Sport (100% linen; 270 yd [247 m]/100 g): #2574 French Blue, 2 (3, 3, 3, 4) skeins.

NEEDLES

BODY—Size U.S. 5 (3.75 mm): straight and a spare needle for three-needle BO.

EDGING—Size U.S. 4 (3.5 mm): straight and double-pointed (dpn).

Adjust needle sizes if necessary to obtain the correct gauge.

NOTIONS

Movable stitch markers (m); several yards of smooth waste yarn for provisional CO; tapestry needle.

GAUGE

21 sts and 24 rows = 4" (10 cm) in St st on larger needles.

Worked in crisp linen, this tunic evokes the 1930s as recorded in Walker Evans's black-and-white photographs. The sleek simplicity of this top is quintessential American Look: functional as well as stylish. It can be dressed up or down.

Back

With larger needles, use a provisional method (see Techniques) to CO 91 (103, 115, 127, 137) sts. Work even in St st (knit on RS, purl on WS) until piece measures 14" (35.5 cm) from beg. Place a movable m into fabric at each end of the needle to mark underarm. Cont working in St st until piece measures 7 (7½, 8, 8¼, 8½)" (18 [19, 20.5, 21, 21.5] cm) from m, ending after a WS row.

Shape Neck

NEXT ROW (RS): K40 (45, 50, 56, 61), BO 11 (13, 15, 15, 15) sts, and work to end—40 (45, 50, 56, 61) sts rem on each side for shoulders. Cont working back and forth on left shoulder sts, keeping right shoulder sts on needle to be worked later.

Shape Left Shoulder with Short-Rows

See Techniques. Purl 1 WS row.

SHORT-ROW 1 (RS): BO 4 (4, 5, 5, 5) sts, knit to last 5 (6, 7, 8, 8) sts, wrap next st, and turn so WS is facing—36 (41, 45, 51, 56) sts rem.

Purl 1 WS row.

SHORT-ROW 2: BO 4 (4, 4, 4, 5) sts, knit to last 10 (12, 14, 16, 16) sts, wrap next st, and turn so WS is facing—32 (37, 41, 47, 51) sts rem.

Purl 1 WS row.

SHORT-ROW 3: BO 4 sts, knit to last 15 (18, 21, 24, 24) sts, wrap next st, and turn so WS is facing—28 (33, 37, 43, 47) sts rem.

Purl 1 WS row.

SHORT-ROW 4: BO 4 sts, knit to last 20 (24, 28, 32, 32) sts, wrap next st, and turn so WS is facing—24 (29, 33, 39, 43) sts rem.

Purl 1 WS row.

NEXT ROW (RS): BO 2 (3, 3, 3, 3) sts and knit to end, picking up the wraps and working them together with the sts they wrap as you come to them—22 (26, 30, 36, 40) sts rem.

Purl 1 WS row. Break yarn and place rem left shoulder sts onto a st holder or waste yarn.

Shape Right Shoulder with Short-Rows

Rejoin yarn to right shoulder sts, preparing to work a WS row.

SHORT-ROW 1 (WS): BO 4 (4, 5, 5, 5) sts, purl to last 5 (6, 7, 8, 8) sts, wrap next st, and turn so RS is facing—36 (41, 45, 51, 56) sts rem.

Knit 1 RS row.

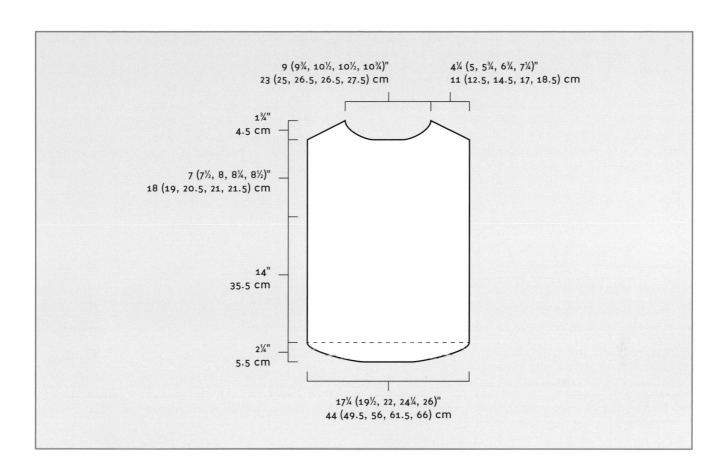

9 (9¾, 10½, 10½, 10¾)"
23 (25, 26.5, 26.5, 27.5) cm

4¼ (5, 5¾, 6¾, 7¼)"
11 (12.5, 14.5, 17, 18.5) cm

1¾"
4.5 cm

7 (7½, 8, 8¼, 8½)"
18 (19, 20.5, 21, 21.5) cm

14"
35.5 cm

2¼"
5.5 cm

17¼ (19½, 22, 24¼, 26)"
44 (49.5, 56, 61.5, 66) cm

SHORT-ROW 2: BO 4 (4, 4, 4, 5) sts, purl to last 10 (12, 14, 16, 16) sts, wrap next st, and turn so RS is facing—32 (37, 41, 47, 51) sts rem.

Knit 1 RS row.

SHORT-ROW 3: BO 4 sts, purl to last 15 (18, 21, 24, 24) sts, wrap next st, and turn so RS is facing—28 (33, 37, 43, 47) sts rem.

Knit 1 RS row.

SHORT-ROW 4: BO 4 sts, purl to last 20 (24, 28, 32, 32) sts, wrap next st, and turn so RS is facing—24 (29, 33, 39, 43) sts rem.

Knit 1 RS row.

NEXT ROW (WS): BO 2 (3, 3, 3, 3) sts and purl to end, picking up the wraps and working them together with the sts they wrap as you come to them—22 (26, 30, 36, 40) sts rem.

Break yarn and place rem sts onto a st holder or waste yarn.

Back Hem

Carefully remove waste yarn from provisional CO and place 91 (103, 115, 127, 137) sts onto larger needles; rejoin yarn, preparing to work a RS row.

Shape Hem with Short-Rows

SHORT-ROW 1 (RS): Knit to last 5 (6, 7, 8, 9) sts, wrap next st, and turn so WS is facing; purl to last 5 (6, 7, 8, 9) sts, wrap next st, and turn so RS is facing.

SHORT-ROW 2 (RS): Knit to last 10 (12, 14, 16, 18) sts, wrap next st, and turn so WS is facing; purl to last 10 (12, 14, 16, 18) sts, wrap next st, and turn so RS is facing.

SHORT-ROW 3: Knit to last 15 (18, 21, 24, 28) sts, wrap next st, and turn so WS is facing; purl to last 15 (18, 21, 24, 28) sts, wrap next st, and turn so RS is facing.

SHORT-ROW 4: Knit to last 20 (24, 28, 32, 36) sts, wrap next st, and turn so WS is facing; purl to last 20 (24, 28, 32, 36) sts, wrap next st, and turn so RS is facing.

SHORT-ROW 5: Knit to last 25 (30, 35, 40, 45) sts, wrap next st, and turn so WS is facing; purl to last 25 (30, 35, 40, 45) sts, wrap next st, and turn so RS is facing.

SHORT-ROW 6: Knit to last 30 (36, 42, 48, 54) sts, wrap next st, and turn so WS is facing; purl to last 30 (36, 42, 48, 54) sts, wrap next st, and turn so RS is facing.

NEXT ROW (RS): Knit to the end, picking up the wraps and working them together with the sts they wrap as they appear.

NEXT ROW (WS): Purl to end picking up the wraps and working them together with the sts they wrap as they appear.

Change to smaller needles.

Applied I-cord

NEXT ROW (RS): K3, k2tog, *slip 4 sts from right needle to left needle, k3, k2tog; rep from * until 8 sts rem (4 sts on each needle). Break yarn, leaving a 12" (30.5 cm) tail. Graft the 4 sts on the right needle together with the 4 sts on the left needle using the Kitchener st (see Techniques).

Front

Work the same as back and back hem.

Finishing

Block pieces to measurements. Return held shoulder sts to needles and, with RS together (WS facing out), join the shoulders with a three-needle BO (see Techniques).

With yarn threaded on a tapestry needle, sew the side seams using a mattress stitch (see Techniques). Sew from the beg of the hem, ending at the movable markers.

Neck Edging

With dpn, use a provisional method to CO 4 sts. Beg at the shoulder with RS facing, *pick up and knit 1 st from the BO neck edge, slip 5 sts from the right needle to the left needle, k3, k2tog; rep from * until the I-cord has been applied around the neck edge to the opposite shoulder and back to the provisional CO.

Break yarn, leaving a 12" (30.5 cm) tail. Carefully remove waste yarn from provisional CO and place 4 sts onto empty dpn. Graft the live sts together using the Kitchener st.

Weave in ends. Block again if desired.

jasper PULLOVER

FINISHED SIZE

About 34½ (39, 44, 48½, 52)" (87.5 [99, 112, 123, 132] cm) bust circumference.

Pullover shown measures 34½" (87.5 cm).

YARN

Sportweight (#2 fine).

SHOWN HERE: Louet Gems Sport (100% merino wool; 225 yd [206 m]/100 g): #2363 Linen Grey (MC), 4 (4, 4, 5, 5) skeins; #2563 Navy (CC), 3 (3, 4, 4, 5) skeins.

NEEDLES

BODY—Size U.S. 5 (3.75 mm): straight and a spare needle for three-needle BO.

EDGING—Size U.S. 4 (3.5 mm): straight and double-pointed (dpn).

Adjust needle sizes if necessary to obtain the correct gauge.

NOTIONS

Movable stitch markers (m); several yards of smooth waste yarn for provisional CO; tapestry needle.

GAUGE

21 sts and 26 rows = 4" (10 cm) in St st on larger needles.

Why seam? Because I've never found a truly jogless way to stripe yarn in the round. In addition to providing stability to a garment made of machine-washable merino wool (which tends to continue to grow bit by bit, over time), working this pullover in pieces and seaming it together with mattress stitch means that the lines match perfectly. Nautical stripes were inspired by the work of iconoclast Jasper Johns.

> **Stitch Guide**
> Stripe Sequence
> (worked over any number of sts)
> **ROWS 1-4:** CC
>
> **ROWS 5-8:** MC
>
> Rep Rows 1–8 for patt.

NOTE: *Because this is layering garment, a small amount a positive ease is recommended.*

Back

With MC and larger needles, use a provisional method (see Techniques) to CO 91 (103, 115, 127, 137) sts. Beg with a WS row, work 3 rows even in St st. Cont working stripe sequence in St st until piece measures 4" (10 cm) from beg, ending after a WS row.

Shape Waist

DEC ROW (RS): K2, k2tog, knit to last 4 sts, ssk, k2–2 sts dec'd.

Work 11 rows even as est, ending after a WS row.

Rep the last 12 rows 2 times–85 (97, 109, 121, 131) sts rem.

Work even in stripe sequence as established for 4 rows, ending after a WS row.

INC ROW (RS): K3, LLI (see Techniques), knit to last 3 sts, RLI (see Techniques), k3–2 sts inc'd.

Work 11 rows even as est, ending after a WS row.

Rep the last 12 rows 2 times–91 (103, 115, 127, 137) sts.

Work even as est until piece measures 17½" (44.5 cm) from beg, ending after a WS row.

Shape Underarm Gusset

INC ROW (RS): K3, LLI, knit to last 3 sts, RLI, k3–2 sts inc'd.

Work 1 WS row as est.

Rep the last 2 rows 5 times–103, (115, 127, 139, 149) sts.

NEXT ROW (RS): Place a movable m into fabric at each end of needle marking underarm and cont working stripe sequence in St st until armhole measures about 7 (7½, 8, 8¼, 8½)" (18 [19, 20.5, 21, 21.5] cm) from m, ending after WS Row 4, 6, or 8 of stripe sequence. Break CC.

Shape Neck

NEXT ROW (RS): With MC, k46 (51, 56, 62, 67), BO 11 (13, 15, 15, 15) sts and work to end–46 (51, 56, 62, 67) sts rem on each side for shoulders. Cont working with MC only back and forth on left shoulder sts, keeping right shoulder sts on needle to be worked later.

Shape Left Shoulder with Short-Rows

See Techniques. Purl 1 WS row.

SHORT-ROW 1 (RS): BO 4 (4, 5, 5, 5) sts, knit to last 8 (8, 8, 8, 10) sts, wrap next st, and turn so WS is facing—42 (47, 51, 57, 62) sts rem.

Purl 1 WS row.

SHORT-ROW 2: BO 4 (4, 4, 4, 5) sts, knit to last 13 (14, 15, 16, 18) sts, wrap next st, and turn so WS is facing—38 (43, 47, 53, 57) sts rem.

Purl 1 WS row.

SHORT-ROW 3: BO 4 sts, knit to last 18 (20, 22, 24, 26) sts, wrap next st, and turn so WS is facing—34 (39, 43, 49, 53) sts rem.

Purl 1 WS row.

SHORT-ROW 4: BO 4 sts, knit to last 23 (26, 29, 32, 34) sts, wrap next st, and turn so WS is facing—30 (35, 39, 45, 49) sts rem.

Purl 1 WS row.

NEXT ROW (RS): BO 2 (3, 3, 3, 3) sts and knit to end, picking up the wraps and working them together with the sts they wrap, as you come to them—28 (32, 36, 42, 46) sts rem.

Purl 1 WS row. Break yarn and place rem left shoulder sts onto a st holder or waste yarn.

Shape Right Shoulder with Short-Rows

Rejoin MC to right shoulder sts, preparing to work a WS row.

SHORT-ROW 1 (WS): BO 4 (4, 5, 5, 5) sts, purl to last 8 (8, 8, 8, 10) sts, wrap next st, and turn so RS is facing—42 (47, 51, 57, 62) sts rem.

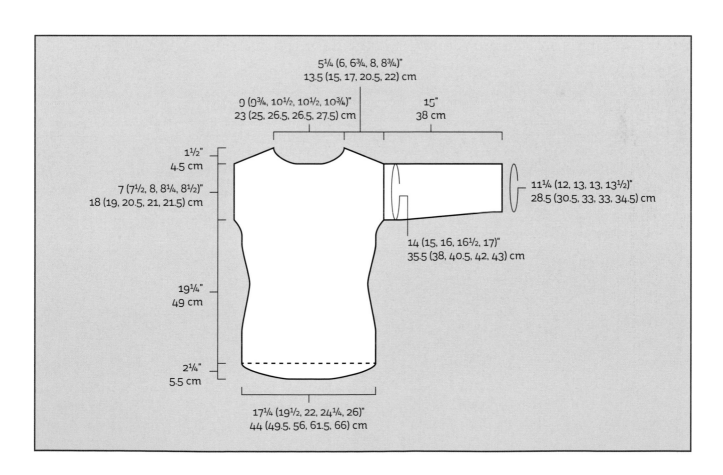

5¼ (6, 6¾, 8, 8¾)"
13.5 (15, 17, 20.5, 22) cm

9 (9¾, 10½, 10½, 10¾)"
23 (25, 26.5, 26.5, 27.5) cm

15"
38 cm

1½"
4.5 cm

7 (7½, 8, 8¼, 8½)"
18 (19, 20.5, 21, 21.5) cm

11¼ (12, 13, 13, 13½)"
28.5 (30.5, 33, 33, 34.5) cm

14 (15, 16, 16½, 17)"
35.5 (38, 40.5, 42, 43) cm

19¼"
49 cm

2¼"
5.5 cm

17¼ (19½, 22, 24¼, 26)"
44 (49.5, 56, 61.5, 66) cm

Knit 1 RS row.

SHORT-ROW 2: BO 4 (4, 4, 4, 5) sts, purl to last 13 (14, 15, 16, 18) sts, wrap next st, and turn so RS is facing—38 (43, 47, 53, 57) sts rem.

Knit 1 RS row.

SHORT-ROW 3: BO 4 sts, purl to last 18 (20, 22, 24, 26) sts, wrap next st, and turn so RS is facing—34 (39, 43, 49, 53) sts rem.

Knit 1 RS row.

SHORT-ROW 4: BO 4 sts, purl to last 23 (26, 29, 32, 34) sts, wrap next st, and turn so RS is facing—30 (35, 39, 45, 49) sts rem.

Knit 1 RS row.

NEXT ROW (WS): BO 2 (3, 3, 3, 3) sts and purl to end, picking up the wraps and working them together with the sts they wrap, as you come to them—28 (32, 36, 42, 46) sts rem.

Break yarn and place rem sts onto a st holder or waste yarn.

Back Hem

Carefully remove waste yarn from provisional CO and place 91 (103, 115, 127, 137) sts onto larger needles; rejoin MC, preparing to work a RS row.

Shape Hem with Short-Rows

SHORT-ROW 1 (RS): Knit to last 5 (6, 7, 8, 9) sts, wrap next st, and turn so WS is facing; purl to last 5 (6, 7, 8, 9) sts, wrap next st, and turn so RS is facing.

SHORT-ROW 2 (RS): Knit to last 10 (12, 14, 16, 18) sts, wrap next st, and turn so WS is facing; purl to last 10 (12, 14, 16, 18) sts, wrap next st, and turn so RS is facing.

SHORT-ROW 3: Knit to last 15 (18, 21, 24, 28) sts, wrap next st, and turn so WS is facing; purl to last 15 (18, 21, 24, 28) sts, wrap next st, and turn so RS is facing.

SHORT-ROW 4: Knit to last 20 (24, 28, 32, 36) sts, wrap next st, and turn so WS is facing; purl to last 20 (24, 28, 32, 36) sts, wrap next st, and turn so RS is facing.

SHORT-ROW 5: Knit to last 25 (30, 35, 40, 45) sts, wrap next st, and turn so WS is facing; purl to last 25 (30, 35, 45) sts, wrap next st, and turn so RS is facing.

SHORT-ROW 6: Knit to last 30 (36, 42, 48, 54) sts, wrap next st, and turn so WS is facing; purl to last 30 (36, 42, 48, 54) sts, wrap next st, and turn so RS is facing.

NEXT ROW (RS): Knit to the end, picking up the wraps and working them together with the sts they wrap as they appear.

NEXT ROW (WS): Purl to end, picking up the wraps and working them together with the sts they wrap as they appear.

Change to smaller needles.

Applied I-cord

NEXT ROW (RS): K3, k2tog, *slip 4 sts from right needle to left needle, k3, k2tog; rep from * until 8 sts rem (4 sts on each needle). Break yarn, leaving a 12" (30.5 cm) tail. Graft the 4 sts on the right needle together with the 4 sts on the left needle using the Kitchener st (see Techniques).

Front

Work the same as back and back hem.

Join Shoulders

Block back and front to measurements.

Return held shoulder sts to needles and, with RS together (WS facing out), join the shoulders with a three-needle BO (see Techniques).

Sleeve

With MC, larger needle, and RS facing, beg at underarm m, pick up and knit 73 (79, 84, 86, 89) sts between markers along the armhole edge.

Beg with a WS row, work 3 rows in St st. Cont working stripe sequence in St st for 6 more rows, ending after a WS row.

Applied I-cord

With smaller dpn, use a provisional method to CO 4 sts. With MC, *k1 from sleeve, slip 5 sts from the right needle to the left needle, *k3, k2tog, slip 4 sts from the right needle to the left needle; rep from * until the I-cord has been applied across all sleeve sts and only 4 sts rem.

Break yarn, leaving a 12" (30.5 cm) tail. Carefully remove waste yarn from provisional CO and place 4 sts onto empty dpn. Graft the live sts together using the Kitchener st.

Work second sleeve the same as the first.

Finishing

With yarn threaded on a tapestry needle, sew the side and sleeve seams using a mattress st (see Techniques).

Neck Edging

With dpn, use a provisional method to CO 4 sts. Beg at the shoulder with RS facing, *pick up and knit 1 st from the BO neck edge, slip 5 sts from the right needle to the left needle, k3, k2tog; rep from * until the I-cord has been applied around the neck edge to the opposite shoulder and back to the provisional CO.

Break yarn, leaving a 12" (30.5 cm) tail. Carefully remove waste yarn from provisional CO and place 4 sts onto empty dpn. Graft the live sts together using the Kitchener st.

Weave in ends. Block again if desired.

Shape Sleeve

DEC ROW (RS): K2, k2tog, knit to last 4 sts, ssk, k2—2 sts dec'd.

Work 11 (9, 9, 7, 7) rows even as est, ending after a WS row.

Rep the last 12 (10, 10, 8, 8) rows 6 (7, 7, 8, 8) times—59 (63, 68, 68, 71) sts rem.

Cont working stripe sequence as est until sleeve measures about 15" (38 cm) from the pick-up row, ending after WS Row 8 of patt. Break MC and CC.

Abbreviations

beg(s)	begin(s); beginning		**psso**	pass slipped stitch over
BO	bind off		**pwise**	purlwise; as if to purl
cir	circular		**rem**	remain(s); remaining
cm	centimeter(s)		**rep**	repeat(s); repeating
cn	cable needle		**rev St st**	reverse stockinette stitch
CO	cast on		**rnd(s)**	round(s)
cont	continue(s); continuing		**RS**	right side
dec(s)('d)	decrease(s); decreasing; decreased		**sl**	slip
dpn	double-pointed needles		**sl st**	slip st (slip stitch purlwise unless otherwise indicated)
foll(s)	follow(s); following		**sl1-k2tog-psso**	slip 1 stitch knitwise, knit 2 stitches together, pass slipped stitch over
g	gram(s)			
inc(s)('d)	increase(s); increasing; increase(d)		**ssk**	slip, slip, knit (decrease)
k	knit		**st(s)**	stitch(es)
k1f&b	knit into the front and back of same stitch		**St st**	stockinette stitch
			tbl	through back loop
k2tog	knit 2 stitches together		**tog**	together
k3tog	knit 3 stitches together		**WS**	wrong side
kwise	knitwise, as if to knit		**wyb**	with yarn in back
m	marker(s)		**wyf**	with yarn in front
mm	millimeter(s)		**yd**	yard(s)
MB	make bobble		**yo**	yarnover
M1	make one (increase)		*****	repeat starting point
oz	ounce		******	repeat all instructions between asterisks
p	purl			
p1f&b	purl into front and back of same stitch		**()**	alternate measurements and/or instructions
p2tog	purl 2 stitches together		**[]**	work instructions as a group a specified number of times
patt(s)	pattern(s)			
pm	place marker			

Techniques

Cast-Ons

Backward-Loop Cast-On

*Loop working yarn and place it on needle backward so that it doesn't unwind. Repeat from *.

Cable Cast-On

If there are no stitches on the needles, make a slipknot of working yarn and place it on the left needle. When there is at least one stitch on the left needle, *use the right needle to knit the first stitch (or slipknot) on left needle *(Figure 1)* and place new loop onto left needle to form a new stitch *(Figure 2)*. Repeat from * for the desired number of stitches, always working into the last stitch made.

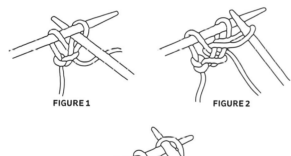

FIGURE 1   FIGURE 2

FIGURE 3

Crochet Chain Provisional Cast-On

With waste yarn and crochet hook, make a loose crochet chain (see below) about four stitches more than you need to cast on. With knitting needle, working yarn, and beginning two stitches from end of chain, pick up and knit one stitch through the back loop of each crochet chain *(Figure 1)* for desired number of stitches. When you're ready to work in the opposite direction, pull out the crochet chain to expose live stitches *(Figure 2)*.

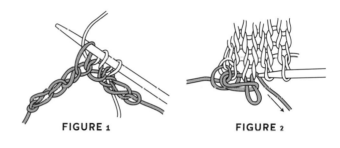

FIGURE 1   FIGURE 2

Crochet

Crochet Chain (ch)

Make a slipknot and place it on the crochet hook if there isn't a loop already on the hook. *Yarn over hook and draw through loop on hook. Repeat from * for desired number of stitches. To fasten off, cut yarn and draw end through last loop formed.

Bind-Offs
I-Cord Bind-Off

With right side facing and using the knitted method, cast on three stitches (for cord) onto the end of the needle holding the stitches to be bound off *(Figure 1)*, *k2, k2tog through back loops (the last cord stitch with the first stitch to be bound off *(Figure 2)*; slip these three stitches back to the left needle *(Figure 3)*, and pull the yarn firmly from the back. Repeat from * until three stitches remain on left needle and no stitches remain on right needle. Bind off remaining stitches using the standard method.

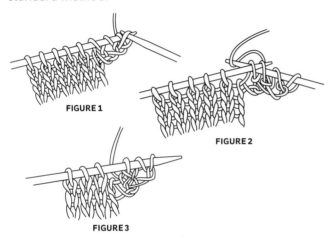

FIGURE 1

FIGURE 2

FIGURE 3

Standard Bind-Off

Knit the first stitch, *knit the next stitch (two stitches on right needle), insert left needle tip into first stitch on right needle *(Figure 1)* and lift this stitch up and over the second stitch *(Figure 2)* and off the needle *(Figure 3)*. Repeat from * for the desired number of stitches.

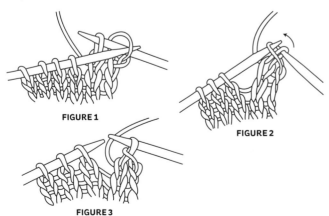

FIGURE 1

FIGURE 2

FIGURE 3

Three-Needle Bind-Off

Place the stitches to be joined onto two separate needles and hold the needles parallel so that the two sides of knitting face together. Insert a third needle into the first stitch on each of two needles *(Figure 1)* and knit them together as one stitch *(Figure 2)*, *knit the next stitch on each needle the same way, then use the left needle tip to lift the first stitch over the second and off the needle *(Figure 3)*. Repeat from * until no stitches remain on first two needles. Cut yarn and pull tail through last stitch to secure.

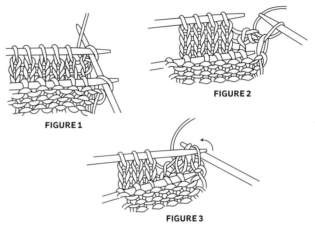

FIGURE 2

FIGURE 1

FIGURE 3

Increases
K1f&b

Knit into a stitch but leave the stitch on the left needle *(Figure 1)*, then knit through the back loop of the same stitch *(Figure 2)* and slip the original stitch off the needle *(Figure 3)*.

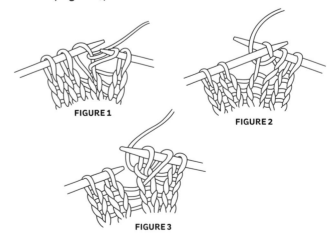

FIGURE 1

FIGURE 2

FIGURE 3

P1f&b

Work as for k1f&b, but purl into the front and back of the same stitch.

Raised Make-One Increase (M1)

This type of increase is characterized by the tiny twisted stitch that forms at the base of the increase. Like the lifted method, it can slant to the right or the left, and you can separate the increases by the desired number of stitches to form a prominent ridge.

For circular yoke shaping, or when no slant is specified, use the slant of your choice.

RIGHT SLANT (M1R): Use the left needle tip to lift the strand between the needle tips from back to front *(Figure 1)*, then knit the lifted loop through the front to twist it *(Figure 2)*.

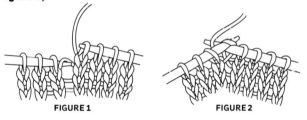

FIGURE 1   FIGURE 2

LEFT SLANT (M1L): Use the left needle tip to lift the strand between the needle tips from front to back *(Figure 1)*, then knit the lifted loop through the back to twist it *(Figure 2)*.

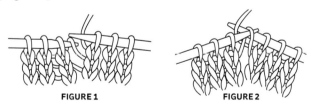

FIGURE 1   FIGURE 2

You can work these increases purlwise (M1P) by purling the lifted strand instead of knitting it.

Lifted Increase (LI)

This type of increase is nearly invisible in the knitting. It can be worked to slant to the right or to the left, which can be used as a design element along raglan shaping. You can separate the increases by the desired number of stitches to form a prominent ridge.

For circular yoke shaping, use the slant of your choice.

RIGHT SLANT (RLI): Knit into the back of the stitch (in the "purl bump") in the row directly below the first stitch on the left needle *(Figure 1)*, then knit the stitch on the needle *(Figure 2)* and slip the original stitch off the needle.

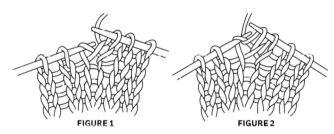

FIGURE 1   FIGURE 2

LEFT SLANT (LLI): Knit the first stitch on the left needle, insert left needle tip into the back of the stitch (in the "purl bump") below the stitch just knitted *(Figure 1)*, then knit this stitch *(Figure 2)*.

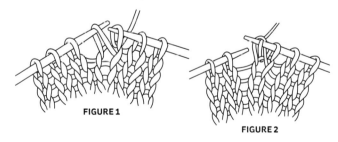

FIGURE 1   FIGURE 2

Decreases

Slip, Slip, Knit (ssk)

Slip two stitches individually knitwise *(Figure 1)*, insert left needle tip into the front of these two slipped stitches, and use the right needle to knit them together through their back loops *(Figure 2)*.

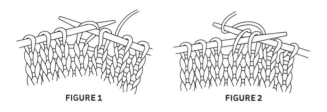

FIGURE 1   **FIGURE 2**

Seams

Mattress Stitch

Place the pieces to be seamed on a table, right sides facing up. Begin at the lower edge and work upward.

Insert threaded needle under one bar between the two edge stitches on one piece, then under the corresponding bar plus the bar above it on the other piece *(Figure 1)*. *Pick up the next two bars on the first piece *(Figure 2)*, then the next two bars on the other *(Figure 3)*. Repeat from *, ending by picking up the last bar or pair of bars on the first piece.

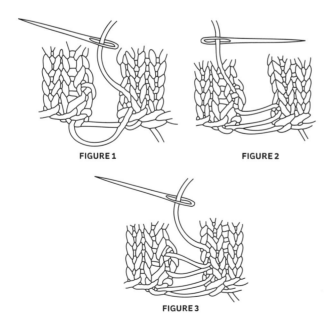

FIGURE 1   **FIGURE 2**

FIGURE 3

Grafting

Kitchener Stitch

Arrange stitches on two needles so that there is the same number of stitches on each needle. Hold the needles parallel to each other with wrong sides of the knitting together. Allowing about ½" (1.3 cm) per stitch to be grafted, thread matching yarn on a tapestry needle. Work from right to left as follows:

STEP 1. Bring tapestry needle through the first stitch on the front needle as if to purl and leave the stitch on the needle *(Figure 1)*.

STEP 2. Bring tapestry needle through the first stitch on the back needle as if to knit and leave that stitch on the needle *(Figure 2)*.

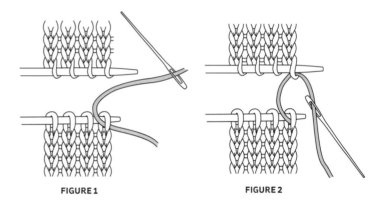

FIGURE 1   **FIGURE 2**

STEP 3. Bring tapestry needle through the first front stitch as if to knit and slip this stitch off the needle, then bring tapestry needle through the next front stitch as if to purl and leave this stitch on the needle *(Figure 3)*.

STEP 4. Bring tapestry needle through the first back stitch as if to purl and slip this stitch off the needle, then bring tapestry needle through the next back stitch as if to knit and leave this stitch on the needle *(Figure 4)*.

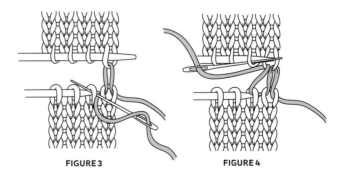

FIGURE 3   **FIGURE 4**

Repeat Steps 3 and 4 until one stitch remains on each needle, adjusting the tension to match the rest of the knitting as you go. To finish, bring tapestry needle through the front stitch as if to knit and slip this stitch off the needle, then bring tapestry needle through the back stitch as if to purl and slip this stitch off the needle.

Short-rows
Knit Side

Work to turning point, slip next stitch purlwise *(Figure 1)*, bring the yarn to the front, then slip the same stitch back to the left needle *(Figure 2)*, turn the work around and bring the yarn in position for the next stitch—one stitch has been wrapped, and the yarn is correctly positioned to work the next stitch. When you come to a wrapped stitch on a subsequent row, hide the wrap by working it together with the wrapped stitch as follows: Insert right needle tip under the wrap (from the front if wrapped stitch is a knit stitch; from the back if wrapped stitch is a purl stitch; *Figure 3*), then into the stitch on the needle, and work the stitch and its wrap together as a single stitch.

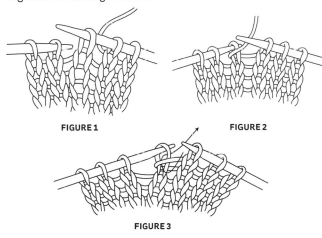

FIGURE 1   FIGURE 2

FIGURE 3

Purl Side

Work to the turning point, slip the next stitch purlwise to the right needle, bring the yarn to the back of the work *(Figure 1)*, return the slipped stitch to the left needle, bring the yarn to the front between the needles *(Figure 2)*, and turn the work so that the knit side is facing—one stitch has been wrapped, and the yarn is correctly positioned to knit the next stitch. To hide the wrap on a subsequent purl row, work to the wrapped stitch, use the tip of the right needle to pick up the wrap from the back, place it on the left needle *(Figure 3)*, then purl it together with the wrapped stitch.

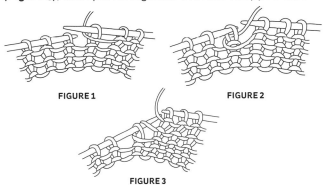

FIGURE 1   FIGURE 2

FIGURE 3

Sewing a Zipper

With RS facing and zipper closed, pin zipper to fronts so front edges cover the zipper teeth. With contrasting thread and RS facing, baste zipper in place close to teeth *(Figure 1)*. Turn work over and with matching sewing thread and needle, stitch outer edges of zipper to WS of fronts *(Figure 2)*, being careful to follow a single column of sts in the knitting to keep zipper straight. Turn work back to RS facing, and with matching sewing thread, sew knitted fabric close to teeth *(Figure 3)*. Remove basting.

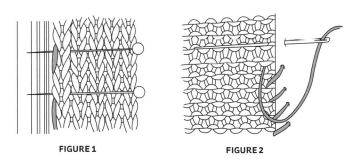

FIGURE 1   FIGURE 2

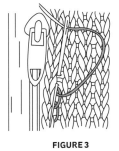

FIGURE 3

Sources for Yarn

Berroco
1 Tupperware Dr., Ste. 4
North Smithfield, RI 02896
(401) 769-1212
berroco.com

Brooklyn Tweed
Brooklyntweed.net

Classic Elite Yarns
16 Esquire Rd., Unit 2
North Billerica, MA 01862
(800) 343-0308
classiceliteyarns.com

Dream in Color
dreamincoloryarn.com

The Fibre Company
Distributed by Kelbourne Woolens
2000 Manor Rd.
Conshohocken, PA 19428
kelbournewoolens.com

Green Mountain Spinnery
Box 568
Putney, VT 05346
(802) 387-4528
spinnery.com

Harrisville Designs
4 Mill Alley
Harrisville, NH 03450
(603) 827-3996

Imperial Stock Ranch Yarn
92462 Hinton Rd.
Maupin, OR 97037
(541) 395-2507
imperialyarn.com

Lorna's Laces
4229 N. Honore St.
Chicago, IL 60613
lornaslaces.net

Louet North America/Gems
3425 Hands Rd.
Prescott, ON
Canada KOE ITO
louet.com

Manos del Uruguay
PO Box 2082
Philadelphia, PA 19103
(888) 566-9970
fairmountfibers.com

O-Wool
Distributed by Tunney Wool Company
915 N. 28th St.
Philadelphia, PA 19130
o-wool.com

Quince and Co.
quinceandco.com

Rowan
*Distributed in the United States
by Westminster Fibers Inc.*
165 Ledge St.
Nashua, NH 03060
westminsterfibers.com

Sincere Sheep
sinceresheep.com

Swans Island
231 Atlantic Hwy. (U.S. Rte. 1)
Northport, ME 04849
(888) 526-9526
swansislandcompany.com

Index

Acknowledgments

Heaps of thanks to everyone who helped make this to happen. To my editors Allison and Erica for all your guidance, to dear friends for all your wisdom and experience. Love and gratitude to my grandmothers for making things, to my dad for art and culture, and to my mother for the courage of my convictions. And to Brett, from the bottom of my heart.

Knit an array of stylish garments & accessories with these inspiring resources from Interweave

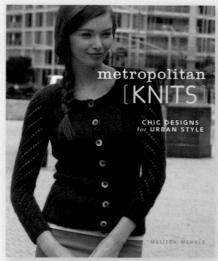

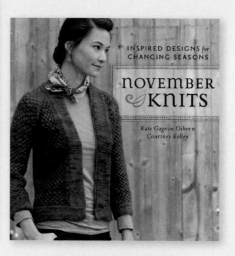

Scarf Style 2
Innovative to Traditional,
25 Fresh Designs to Knit
Ann Budd
ISBN 978-1-59668-781-3, $24.95

Metropolitan Knits
Chic Designs for Urban Style
Melissa Wehrle
ISBN 978-1-59668-778-3, $24.95

November Knits
Inspired Designs
for Changing Seasons
Kate Gagnon Osborn
and Courtney Kelley
ISBN 978-1-59668-439-3, $24.95

Available at your favorite retailer or knitting daily *shop* shop.knittingdaily.com

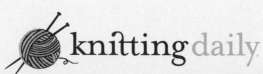

Join Knittingdaily.com, an online community that shares your passion for knitting. You'll get a free eNewsletter, free patterns, projects store, a daily blog, event updates, galleries, tips and techniques, and more. Sign up for *Knitting Daily* at **Knittingdaily.com.**

KNITS

INTERWEAVE

From cover to cover, *Interweave Knits* magazine presents great projects for the beginner to the advanced knitter. Every issue is packed full of captivating smart designs, step-by-step instructions, easy-to-understand illustrations, plus well-written, lively articles sure to inspire. **Interweaveknits.com**